knitted animal
socks and hats

35 furry and friendly creatures
to keep you warm

Fiona Goble

CICO BOOKS
LONDON NEW YORK

Published in 2018 by CICO Books
An imprint of Ryland Peters & Small Ltd
20–21 Jockey's Fields   341 E 116th St
London   New York
WC1R 4BW   NY 10029

www.rylandpeters.com

10 9 8 7 6 5 4 3 2 1

Text © Fiona Goble 2018
Design, illustration, and photography
© CICO Books 2018

A CIP catalog record for this book is
available from the Library of Congress and
the British Library.

ISBN: 978 1 78249 640 3

Printed in China

Editor: Kate Haxell
Designer: Geoff Borin
Photographer: Terry Benson
Stylist: Jess Contomichalos
Illustrator: Stephen Dew

Art director: Sally Powell
Production controller: Mai-Ling Collyer
Publishing manager: Penny Craig
Publisher: Cindy Richards

contents

introduction

Whether you're after a pair of tiger socks to keep your feet looking fabulous on a chilly evening, or a cute raccoon hat for a new baby, you're in the right place. This collection of animal-themed knits will keep heads and feet cozy and looking good, and there are projects to fit all the family.

All the hats in the book are knitted on standard knitting needles, though it would be quite straightforward to adapt the patterns and knit them on a circular needle, if you prefer knitting this way and have adapted patterns before. Most of the socks are worked on a set of four needles that have points at both ends. These are usually called "double-pointed needles"—or "dpns" for short. I don't recommend knitting socks on a circular needle because the patterns include specific instructions for needle 1, needle 2, and so on, and adapting the pattern would be quite complicated.

When I was new to knitting, nothing seemed more daunting than knitting on a set of four double-pointed needles. Firstly, it meant you could drop stitches at both ends of your needles! And if that wasn't bad enough, you had to use double the number of needles you were used to working with. But I promise, it doesn't take long

to get used to them. And one of the benefits of knitting on four needles is that it creates a tube of knitting, so there is very little sewing together to do.

If you've never knitted on four needles before, I recommend you look at the instructions for knitting in the round on page 121 and practice with some scrap yarn before starting your project. This way, you won't have to stop to figure out the basics when you're in the middle of things. For more information, take a look at the rest of the section on knitting socks on page 121, where I have some useful advice for newbie sock knitters, including working the heel part of the socks.

Please bear in mind that if you fall in love with a pair of socks but they look either a little short or long—although the width looks fine—you can easily adapt the pattern by knitting a few rows more or a few rows less in the leg and/or foot part of the sock. But remember you may need to buy more yarn if you're making them longer.

Most of the projects are reasonably straightforward to knit and some are suitable for almost complete beginners. I've ranked the projects according to the level of skills required, from one to three symbols. Those with one symbol should be well within the scope of "beginner knitters" and those with two symbols should be within the scope of "intermediate knitters". The projects marked with three stars should also be within the scope of "intermediate knitters" but are slightly more complex. Whatever project you choose, it's a good idea to check through the instructions before buying your yarn, to make absolutely sure you feel confident.

Although I've recommended particular yarns for each project, most of these can be quite easily substituted if you can't find the particular yarn in your country. For more information, check out the very useful website called yarnsub.com.

Finally, if you have any comments or queries, please feel free to contact me via my website, fionagoble.com, where I will always do my best to help out. I've had great fun creating the projects in this book and I hope you love making and wearing your own versions.

Fiona Goble

CHAPTER 1

little ones

teddy booties

Teddy bears—named after the bear-loving USA President Teddy Roosevelt—have become a childhood classic. So what could be more perfect snuggled around a baby's little feet than these warm and fuzzy teddy booties? They're knitted flat, on straight needles, in a yarn that comes in lots of lovely colors. I've chosen a classic gold, but I think they'd look great in pastel shades, too. The choice, as always, is up to you.

YARN AND MATERIALS

Katia Peru (40% wool, 40% acrylic, 20% alpaca), 115yd (106m) per 3½oz (100g) ball of bulky (chunky) yarn

  1 ball in 039 (A)

Oddment of light worsted (DK) yarn in black (B)

NEEDLES AND EQUIPMENT

Pair of US8 (5mm) knitting needles

Stitch holder

Yarn sewing needle

Large-eyed embroidery needle

SIZE

To fit an average baby 0–6 (6–12) months

(For more information on sizes, see page 112)

Actual measurements: length approx. 3½in/8.25cm (4in/10cm)

GAUGE (TENSION)

17 sts and 20 rows to 4in (10cm) square over stockinette (stocking) stitch on US8 (5mm) needles

ABBREVIATIONS

See page 127

Main bootie

(Make 2)

Cast on 22(24) sts.

Smaller size only

Row 1: K2, [p2, k2] to end.
Row 2: P2, [k2, p2] to end.
Rep last 2 rows twice more.

Larger size only

Row 1: [K2, p2] to end.
Rep last row 5 times more.

Both sizes

Row 7: K15(16), turn.
Row 8: P8, turn.
Row 9: Sl1 pwise WYB, k to end.
Row 10: Sl1 pwise, p to end.
Rep rows 9–10, twice (3 times) more.
Leave sts on holder and break yarn.
With RS facing, rejoin yarn to right-hand edge at base of rectangle just worked, at inner edge of 7(8) sts on needle. Pick up and knit 5(6) sts up first side, k8 sts on holder, pick up and knit 5(6) sts down second side, k rem 7(8) sts. *(32/36 sts)*
Work 3 rows in st st beg with a p row.
Next row: K3, k2tog, k to last 5 sts, ssk, k3. *(30/34 sts)*
Next row: Knit.
Rep last 2 rows once more. *(28/32 sts)*
Next row: K3, k2tog, k5(7), ssk, k4, k2tog, k5(7), ssk, k3. *(24/28 sts)*
Next row: Knit.
Next row: K3, k2tog, k3(5), ssk, k4, k2tog, k3(5), ssk, k3. *(20/24 sts)*
Bind (cast) off kwise.

Ear

(Make 4)

Cast on 4 sts.

Row 1: Knit.
Row 2: Ssk, k2tog. *(2 sts)*
Row 3: K2tog. *(1 st)*
Fasten off.

To make up

Sew back and sole seam using flat stitch (see page 126).
Stitch the ears in position, using the photograph as a guide.
Using B, work two French knots (see page 124) for the eyes.
Using B again, work a small coil of chain stitch (see page
124) for the nose and add a small vertical stitch just below it.
Weave in all loose ends.

unicorn socks

These mythical animals have featured in folklore for hundreds of years, and if you love all things full of hope and wonder, you're bound to be a big unicorn fan. I've chosen two shades of pink for these unicorns, but if you want something less girlie, it won't matter at bit. After all, they're creatures of legend, so you really can knit and decorate them in any colors that take your fancy.

YARN AND MATERIALS

Cascade 220 Fingering (100% wool), 273yd (250m) per 1¾oz (50g) ball of fingering (4ply) yarn

    1 ball in Cerise 7802 (A)
    3 balls in Tutu 9477 (B)
    1 ball in White 8505 (C)

Oddment of light worsted (DK) yarn in black (D)

Oddments of light worsted (DK) yarns in pastel shades —I used shades 001 Primrose, 002 Apple, and 071 Pool from Debbie Bliss Baby Cashmerino (53% wool, 33% acrylic, 12% cashmere)

NEEDLES AND EQUIPMENT

Set of 4 US6 (4mm) double-pointed knitting needles

Set of 4 US5 (3.75mm) double-pointed knitting needles

Pair of US5 (3.75mm) knitting needles

USF-5 (3.75mm) crochet hook or one of similar size

Stitch holder (optional)

Stitch marker

Yarn sewing needle

Large-eyed embroidery needle

SIZE

To fit a child 2–4 (4–6) years

(For more information on sizes, see page 112)

Actual measurements: approx. 5in/13cm (6in/15cm) from toe to heel (unstretched)

GAUGE (TENSION)

22 sts and 28 rows to 4in (10cm) square over stockinette (stocking) stitch on US5 (3.75mm) needles, using yarn double

ABBREVIATIONS

See page 127

Main sock

(Make 2)
Using set of US6 (4mm) needles, cast on 40(44) sts in A.
Round 1: [K2, p2] to end.
Rep round 1, 9 times more.
Break A, join in B, and change to set of US5 (3.75mm) needles.
Knit 40(48) rounds.

HEEL

Next row: K10(11), turn.
Next row: P20(22), turn.
Work rem of heel on 20(22) sts just worked, leaving rem 20(22) sts for instep on stitch holder or spare needle.
Work 8(10) rows in st st beg with a k row.
Next row: K12(13), ssk, k1, turn.
Next row: Sl1 pwise, p5, p2tog, p1, turn.
Next row: Sl1 pwise, k to 1 st before gap, ssk, k1, turn.
Next row: Sl1 pwise, p to 1 st before gap, p2tog, p1, turn.
Rep last 2 rows once(twice) more. *(14 sts)*
Smaller size only
Next row: Sl1 pwise, k to st before gap, ssk, turn.
Next row: Sl1 pwise, p to last 2 sts, p2tog. *(12 sts)*

Both sizes
HEEL GUSSET

 On needle 1: K all 12(14) heel sts and pick up and knit 7(8) sts up side of heel flap and 1 st from instep sts.
On needle 2: K 18(20) instep sts.
On needle 3: K rem st from instep, pick up and knit 7(8) sts up side of heel flap and k 6(7) sts from heel. *(46/52 sts)*
Put marker on next st to mark beg of round.
Next round: On needle 1, k to last 3 sts, k2tog, k1; on needle 2, k all sts; on needle 3, k1, ssk, k rem sts. *(44/50 sts)*
Next round: Knit.
Rep last 2 rounds 10 times more. *(34/40 sts)*

FOOT

Knit 8(12) rounds.
Next round (ridge): Purl.

TOE

Break B, join in C.
Next round: On needle 1, k to last 3 sts, k2tog, k1; on needle 2, k1, ssk, k to last 3 sts, k2tog, k1; on needle 3, k1, ssk, k to end of round. *(30/36 sts)*
Next round: Knit.
Rep last 2 rounds once more. *(26/32 sts)*
Next round: On needle 1, k to last 3 sts, k2tog, k1; on needle 2, k1, ssk, k to last 3 sts, k2tog, k1; on needle 3, k1, ssk, k to end of round. *(22/28 sts)*
Rep last round 4(5) times more. *(6/8 sts)*
Break yarn, thread through rem sts, and secure.

Ear

(Make 8)
Using straight US5 (3.75mm) needles, cast on 6 sts in B.
Work 4 rows in st st beg with a k row.
Row 5: Ssk, k2, k2tog. *(4 sts)*
Row 6: Purl.
Row 7: Ssk, k2tog. *(2 sts)*
Row 8: P2tog. *(1 st)*
Fasten off.

Horn

(Make 2)
Using standard US5 (3.75mm) needles, cast on 8 sts in C.
Work 4 rows in st st beg with a k row.
Row 5: K2tog, k to last 2 sts, ssk. *(6 sts)*
Work 3 rows in st st beg with a p row.
Row 9: K2tog, k2, ssk. *(4 sts)*
Row 10: Purl.
Row 11: K2tog, ssk. *(2 sts)*
Row 12: P2tog. *(1 st)*
Fasten off.

Forelock

Using the crochet hook, work two 5-in (13-cm) crochet chains (see page 123) in each of the three pastel yarns.

To make up

For the eyes, use a divided thread of D to embroider a small coil in chain stitch (see page 124) and work a circle of chain stitch around the coil using a double strand of B. For nostrils, work two French knots in D (see page 124).
For the horn, sew the back seams and stuff lightly with some scrap yarn. Using a single strand of A, work a spiral of chain stitch around the horn, using the photograph as a guide.
For the ears, pair up pieces, seam the sides, and sew in place using the photograph as a guide.
Stitch the forelock crochet chains in place just below the horn.

pug hat

With their wrinkly faces, bright eyes, and friendly nature, it's no wonder people love these cute little dogs. They are one of the oldest breeds in the world and originally came from China. If you want to grab a bit of pug style for the child in your life, now's your chance. The hat is knitted in an easy-to-wear wool and acrylic mix and I've added shiny button eyes, but you could just as easily embroider the eyes using black yarn.

YARN AND MATERIALS

Cascade Pacific Chunky (60% acrylic, 40% wool), 120yd (110m) per 3½oz (100g) ball of bulky (chunky) yarn

    1 ball in Espresso 42 (A)
    1 ball in Latte 30 (B)

Oddment of light worsted (DK) yarn in black (C)

2 x ⅝in (16mm) shiny black shank buttons

NEEDLES AND EQUIPMENT

Pair of US9 (5.5mm) knitting needles

Yarn sewing needle

Large-eyed embroidery needle

SIZE

To fit a child 4–5 (6–7) years

(For more information on sizes, see page 112)

Actual measurements: approx. 16¼in/41cm (17¾in/45cm) circumference (unstretched)

GAUGE (TENSION)

16 sts and 19 rows to a 4in (10cm) square over stockinette (stocking) stitch using US9 (5.5mm) needles

ABBREVIATIONS

See page 127

Main hat

(Make 1)
Cast on 66(72) sts in A.
Knit 4 rows.
Break yarn.
Row 5: Join in B and k21(24); rejoin A and k24; using B from center of ball, k to end.
Row 6: P22(25) in B, p22 in A, p in B to end.
Row 7: K23(26) in B, k20 in A, k in B to end.
Row 8: P24(27) in B, p18 in A, p in B to end.
Row 9: K25(28) in B, k16 in A, k in B to end.
Row 10: P25(28) in B, p16 in A, p in B to end.

Row 11: K26(29) in B, k14 in A, k in B to end.
Row 12: P26(29) in B, p14 in A, p in B to end.
Row 13: K27(30) in B, k12 in A, k in B to end.
Row 14: P28(31) in B, p10 in A, p in B to end.
Row 15: K29(32) in B, k8 in A, k in B to end.
Break A and B from outside of ball, and work rem of main hat in B.
Work 11(13) rows in st st beg with a p row.
Larger size only
Next row: K5, [k2tog, k10] 5 times, k2tog, k5. *(66 sts)*
Next row: Purl.
Both sizes
Next row: K4, [sl2, k1, p2sso, k8] 5 times, sl2, k1, p2sso, k4. *(54 sts)*
Next and every WS row unless stated otherwise: Purl.
Next RS row: K3, [sl2, k1, p2sso, k6] 5 times, sl2, k1, p2sso, k3. *(42 sts)*
Next RS row: K2, [sl2, k1, p2sso, k4] 5 times, sl2, k1, p2sso, k2. *(30 sts)*
Next RS row: K1, [sl2, k1, p2sso, k2] 5 times, sl2, k1, p2sso, k1. *(18 sts)*
Next row (WS): [P2tog] to end. *(9 sts)*
Break yarn leaving a long tail. Thread yarn tail through rem sts, pull up tightly, and secure.

Eye patches

(Make 2)
Cast on 2 sts in A.
Row 1: [Inc] twice. *(4 sts)*
Row 2 and every WS row unless stated otherwise: Purl.
Row 3: [Inc, k1] twice. *(6 sts)*
Row 5: Knit.
Row 7: Ssk, k2, k2tog. *(4 sts)*
Row 9: Ssk, k2tog. *(2 sts)*
Row 10: P2tog. *(1 st)*
Fasten off.

Ear

(Make 2)
Cast on 6 sts in A.
Row 1: Inc, k3, inc, k1. *(8 sts)*
Work 5 rows in st st beg with a p row.
Row 7: K1, ssk, k2, k2tog, k1. *(6 sts)*
Row 8: Purl.
Row 9: K1, ssk, k2tog, k1. *(4 sts)*
Row 10: Purl.
Row 11: Ssk, k2tog. *(2 sts)*
Row 12: P2tog. *(1 st)*
Fasten off.

To make up

Using B, work a line of chain stitch (see page 124) around the top of the muzzle, using the photograph as a guide for all features.
Sew eye patches in place just above the muzzle. Stitch buttons in place for eyes. Using a double strand of B, work a curved line in chain stitch near the eye, beginning at the muzzle.
Stitch the base of the ears in place. Curve them gently then secure the tips in place on the main hat.
Using C, work a coil of chain stitch in a soft upside-down triangle shape for the nose. Add the cleft and mouth in chain stitch.
Sew the back seam using flat stitch (see page 126).
Weave in all loose ends.

dinosaur socks

Dinosaurs are no longer roaming the earth—but they're alive and kicking in the imaginations of children all over the world. So I could hardly compile a book on animal socks and hats without them. I've chosen a classic green look for this pair, but feel free to customize. Some scientists really do believe that dinosaurs could have been purple, orange, red, or even yellow with blue spots!

YARN AND MATERIALS

Red Heart Lovely Wool (55% wool, 25% acrylic, 20% nylon), 131yd (120m) per 1¾oz (50g) ball of light worsted (DK) yarn

    1 ball in Mallard 06203 (A)
    2 balls in Apple 06125 (B)

Oddment of light worsted (DK) yarn in black (C)

Oddment of light worsted (DK) yarn in mauve (D)

Oddment of light worsted (DK) yarn in white (E)

NEEDLES AND EQUIPMENT

Set of 4 US6 (4mm) double-pointed knitting needles

Set of 4 US5 (3.75mm) double-pointed knitting needles

Pair of US5 (3.75mm) knitting needles

Stitch holder (optional)

Stitch marker

Yarn sewing needle

Large-eyed embroidery needle

SIZE

To fit a child 2–4 (4–6) years

(For more information on sizes, see page 112)

Actual measurements: approx. 5in/13cm (6¾in/17cm) from toe to heel (unstretched)

GAUGE (TENSION)

22 sts and 28 rows to 4in (10cm) square over stockinette (stocking) stitch on US5 (3.75mm) needles

ABBREVIATIONS

See page 127

Main sock

(Make 2)
Using set of US6 (4mm) needles, cast on 36(40) sts in A.
Round 1: [K2, p2] to end, placing marker on 1st st of round.
Rep round 1, 7 times more.
Break A, join in B, and change to set of US5 (3.75mm) needles.
Knit 40(46) rounds.

HEEL

Using B, k9(10), turn.
Break B and join in A.
Next row: P18(20), turn.
Work rem of heel on 18(20) sts just worked, leaving rem 18(20) sts for instep on stitch holder or spare needle.
Next row: [Sl1 pwise WYB, k1] to end.
Next row: Sl1 pwise, p to end.
Rep last 2 rows 8(9) times more.
Next row: K11(12), ssk, k1, turn.
Next row: Sl1 pwise, p5, p2tog, p1, turn.
Next row: Sl1 pwise, k to 1 st before gap, ssk, k1, turn.
Next row: Sl1 pwise, p to 1 st before gap, p2tog, p1, turn.
Rep last 2 rows once more. *(12/14 sts)*
Larger size only
Next row: Sl1 pwise, k to st before gap, ssk, turn.
Next row: Sl1 pwise, p to last 2 sts, p2tog. *(12 sts)*

Both sizes
HEEL GUSSET

On needle 1: Using B, k across all heel sts and pick up and knit 9(10) sts up side of heel flap.
On needle 2: K all 18(20) instep sts.
On needle 3: Pick up and knit 9(10) sts up side of heel flap and k 6 of heel sts. *(48/52 sts)*
Put marker on next st to mark beg of round.
Next round: On needle 1, k to last 3 sts, k2tog, k1; on needle 2, k all sts; on needle 3, k1, ssk, k to end. *(46/50 sts)*
Next round: Knit.
Rep last 2 rounds 5 times more. *(36/40 sts)*

FOOT

Knit 8(16) rounds.

TOE

Round 1: On needle 1, k to last 3 sts, k2tog, k1; on needle 2, k1, ssk, k to last 3 sts, k2tog, k1; on needle 3, k1, ssk, k to end. *(32/36 sts)*
Round 2: Knit.
Rep rounds 1–2 once more. *(28/32 sts)*
Round 5: On needle 1, k to last 3 sts, k2tog, k1; on needle 2, k1, ssk, k to last 3 sts, k2tog, k1; on needle 3, k1, ssk, k to end. *(24/28 sts)*
Rep round 5, 4(5) times more. *(8 sts)*
Break yarn, thread through rem sts, and secure.

Spines

(Make 2 sets)
Using straight US5 (3.75mm) needles, cast on 8 sts in A.
Row 1: Sl1, k to end.
Row 2: K2tog, k to end. *(7 sts)*
Rep rows 1–2, 3 times more. *(4 sts)*
Row 9: Sl1, k to end.
Row 10: Cast on 4 sts, k all sts.
Rep rows 1–10, twice (3 times) more.
Rep rows 1–9 once more. *(4 sts)*
Next row: K2tog, k to end. *(3 sts)*
Next row: Sl1, k to end.
Next row: K2tog, k1. *(2 sts)*
Next row: K2tog. *(1 st)*
Fasten off.

To make up

Sew spine pieces in place down the back of each sock, cast on edge to heel, between heel and ribbed top.
For the eyes, use C to embroider a small coil in chain stitch (see page 124) and work two circles of chain stitch around this coil using B. For the nostrils, work two French knots (see page 124) in C and work a circle of chain stitch around these in B. For the mouth, work a line of chain stitch in D, using the photograph as a guide. Work single chain stitches for the teeth using E.
Weave in all loose ends.

piglet socks

Piglets are so clever they can recognize their mother's voice and even their own names, so I thought piggy socks would be a brilliant addition to this collection. I chose a superfine merino wool in a lovely shade of peachy pink, and I think these socks make a beautiful gift for any fashion-conscious baby who wants to stand out from the crowd.

YARN AND MATERIALS

Sugar Bush Yarns Crisp (100% wool), 95yd (87m) per 1¾oz (50g) of light worsted (DK) yarn

1(2) ball(s) in Provincial Peach 2025 (A)

Oddment of light worsted (DK) in dark gray (B)

NEEDLES AND EQUIPMENT

Set of 4 US5 (3.75mm) double-pointed knitting needles

Stitch holder (optional)

Yarn sewing needle

Large-eyed embroidery needle

SIZE

To fit a baby 0–6 (9–12) months

(For more information on sizes, see page 112)

Actual measurements: approx. 4¼in/10.5cm (5in/13cm) from toe to heel (unstretched)

GAUGE (TENSION)

20 sts and 28 rows to 4in (10cm) square over stockinette (stocking) stitch on US5 (3.75mm) needles

ABBREVIATIONS

See page 127

Main sock

(Make 2)
Cast on 25(29) sts.
Round 1: Knit.
Round 2: Purl.
Rep rounds 1–2 once more.
Knit 22(28) rounds.

HEEL

Next row: K6(7), turn.
Next row: P12(14), turn.
Work rem of heel on 12(14) sts just worked, leaving rem 13(15) sts for instep on stitch holder or spare needle.
Work 10 rows in st st beg with a k row.
Next row: WYB, sl1 pwise, k6(8), ssk, k1, turn.
Next row: Sl1 pwise, p3(5), p2tog, p1, turn.

Next row: WYB, sl1 pwise, k to st before gap, ssk, k1, turn.
Next row: Sl1 pwise, p to st before gap, p2tog, p1, turn. *(8/10 sts)*

HEEL GUSSET
On needle 1: K across all sts on heel, pick up and knit 5(6) sts up side of heel.
On needle 2: K all instep sts.
On needle 3: Pick up and knit 5(6) sts down second side of heel, k4(5). *(31/37 sts)*
Next round: On needle 1, k to last 3 sts, k2tog, k1; on needle 2, k; on needle 3, k1, ssk, k to end of round. *(29/35 sts)*
Next round: Knit.
Rep last 2 rounds 3 times more. *(23/29 sts)*

FOOT
Knit 8(12) rounds.

TOE
Round 1: On needle 1, k to last 3 sts, k2tog, k1; on needle 2, k1, ssk, k to last 3 sts, k2tog, k1; on needle 3, k1, ssk, k to end. *(19/25 sts)*
Round 2: Knit.
Rep rounds 1–2 once more. *(15/21 sts)*
Round 5: On needle 1, k to last 3 sts, k2tog, k1; on needle 2, k1, ssk, k to last 3 sts, k2tog, k1; on needle 3, k1, ssk, k to end. *(11/17 sts)*
Rep round 5, once (twice) more. *(7/9 sts)*
Break yarn, thread through rem sts, and secure.

Ear

(Make 8)
Cast on 4 sts.
Work 3 rows in st st beg with a k row.
Row 4: P2tog, p2tog tbl. *(2 sts)*
Row 5: K2tog. *(1 st)*
Row 6: Inc pwise. *(2 sts)*
Row 7: [Inc] twice. *(4 sts)*
Work 3 rows in st st beg with a p row.
Bind (cast) off.

Snout

(Make 2)
Cast on 4 sts.
Row 1: [Inc, k1] twice. *(6 sts)*
Row 2: Purl.
Row 3: Ssk, k2, k2tog. *(4 sts)*
Bind (cast) off pwise.

To make up

Sew two ear pieces together to make each ear. Sew the ears in place on the main sock, using the photograph as a guide.
For each eye, use B to work two straight stitches (see page 124) in a flattened V shape.
Sew the snout in place, stuffing it with the yarn tails to give it a little dimension as you go.
For the nostrils, use B to work two French knots (see page 124).
Weave in all loose ends.

arctic fox hat

Arctic foxes live in some of the coldest places on Earth, where their thick fur keeps them warm. The foxes are usually pure white in winter, which makes it hard for their enemies to spot them, and in summer, their fur turns a little grayish-brown—like this one—to make sure they stay camouflaged when the snow begins to melt. When the temperature in your town feels like the Arctic, this hat, knitted in pure wool, is sure to keep its owner super-cozy.

YARN AND MATERIALS

Cascade 128 Superwash (100% wool), 126yd (116m) per 3½oz (100g) ball of bulky (chunky) yarn

    1 ball in Feather Grey 875 (A)
    1 ball in White 871 (B)

Oddment of light worsted (DK) yarn in black (C)

NEEDLES AND EQUIPMENT

Pair of US9 (5.5mm) knitting needles

Yarn sewing needle

Large-eyed embroidery needle

Nylon brush, such as a toothbrush (optional)

SIZE

To fit a child 4–5 (6–7) years

(For more information on sizes, see page 112)

Actual measurements: approx. 16¼in/41cm (17¾in/45cm) circumference (unstretched)

GAUGE (TENSION)

16 sts and 19 rows to 4in (10cm) square over stockinette (stocking) stitch using US9 (5.5mm) needles

ABBREVIATIONS

See page 127

Main hat

(Make 1)
Before you begin, wind off a few yards (meters) of A into a separate small ball.
Cast on 66(72) sts in A from main ball.
Row 1: [K1, p1] to end.
Rep row 1, 3 times more.
Row 5: Purl.
Row 6: K18(21) in A, join in B and k14, join in A from small ball and k2, join in B from center of ball and k14, join in A from center of ball and k in A to end.
Row 7: P18(21) in A, p14 in B, p2 in A, p14 in B, p in A to end.
Row 8: K18(21) in A, k13 in B, k4 in A, k13 in B, k in A to end.
Row 9: P18(21) in A, p13 in B, p4 in A, p13 in B, p in A to end.
Row 10: K18(21) in A, k12 in B, k6 in A, k12 in B, k in A to end.
Row 11: P18(21) in A, p12 in B, p6 in A, p12 in B, p in A to end.
Row 12: K18(21) in A, k11 in B, k8 in A, k11 in B, k in A to end.
Row 13: P18(21) in A, p10 in B, p10 in A, p10 in B, p in A to end.
Row 14: K18(21) in A, k9 in B, k12 in A, k9 in B, k in A to end.
Row 15: P18(21) in A, p8 in B, p14 in A, p8 in B, p in A to end.
Row 16: K18(21) in A, k7 in B, k16 in A, k7 in B, k in A to end.
Break all yarns except leading A.
Work 9(11) rows in st st beg with a p row.
Larger size only
Next row: K5, [k2tog, k10] 5 times, k2tog, k5. *(66 sts)*
Next row: Purl.
Both sizes
Next row: K4, [sl2, k1, p2sso, k8] 5 times, sl2, k1, p2sso, k4. *(54 sts)*
Next and every WS row unless stated otherwise: Purl.

ARCTIC FOX HAT 23

Next RS row: K3, [sl2, k1, p2sso, k6] 5 times, sl2, k1, p2sso, k3. *(42 sts)*
Next RS row: K2, [sl2, k1, p2sso, k4] 5 times, sl2, k1, p2sso, k2. *(30 sts)*
Next RS row: K1, [sl2, k1, p2sso, k2] 5 times, sl2, k1, p2sso, k1. *(18 sts)*
Next row (WS): [P2tog] to end. *(9 sts)*
Break yarn leaving a long tail. Thread yarn tail through rem sts, pull up tightly, and secure.

Ear

(Make 4, 2 in A and 2 in B)
Cast on 12 sts.
Row 1: Knit.
Row 2: Purl.
Row 3: K1, ssk, k to last 3 sts, k2tog, k1. *(10 sts)*
Beg with a p row, work 3 rows in st st.
Rep rows 3–6 (last 4 rows) once more. *(8 sts)*
Row 11: K1, ssk, k2, k2tog, k1. *(6 sts)*
Row 12: Purl.
Row 13: K1, ssk, k2tog, k1. *(4 sts)*
Row 14: [P2tog] twice. *(2 sts)*
Row 15: K2tog. *(1 st)*
Fasten off.

To make up

Sew back seam using flat stitch (see page 126).
Place one ear piece in A and one in B right sides together. Oversew (see page 125) along sides. Turn right side out and join lower seam. Repeat for second ear. Oversew the ears in position along the front and back of lower seam, using the photograph as a guide. Using a double strand of A, work a row of chain stitch (see page 124) along the sides of the ear fronts, just to the front of the side seam. Using C, work a length of chain stitch for the eyes and work a coil of chain stitch for the nose.
Weave in all loose ends.
Using the small nylon brush, dampen then brush the face lightly to give it a slightly fuzzy look.

dinosaur hat

Every self-respecting child falls in love with dinosaurs at some time in their life, so why not prepare them for it with this cool, toddler-sized dino-hat? The wool-rich yarn I've used comes in a range of brilliant colors, including lots of pinks, greens, and blues, and I do love this zingy orange. But feel free to customize the headgear to suit its proud owner.

YARN AND MATERIALS

Cascade Pacific Chunky (60% acrylic, 40% wool), 120yd (110m) per 3½oz (100g) ball of bulky (chunky) yarn

    1 ball in Persimmon 84 (A)

Cascade 220 Sport (100% wool), 164yd (150m) per 1¾oz (50g) ball of light worsted (DK) yarn

    1 ball in Christmas Red 8895 (B)

Oddment of bulky (chunky) yarn in white (C)

Oddment of light worsted (DK) yarn in black (D)

Small handful of polyester toy filling

NEEDLES AND EQUIPMENT

Pair of US9 (5.5mm) knitting needles

Pair of US8 (5mm) knitting needles

US9 (5.5mm) circular knitting needle

Yarn sewing needle

Large-eyed embroidery needle

2 x stitch markers or small safety pins

SIZE

To fit a toddler 12–18 months (2–3 years)

(For more information on sizes, see page 112)

Actual measurements: approx. 15in/38cm (16¾in/42.5cm) circumference (unstretched)

GAUGE (TENSION)

14 sts and 20 rows to 4in (10cm) square over stockinette (stocking) stitch on US9 (5.5mm) needles

ABBREVIATIONS

See page 127

Main hat

(Make 1)

Using US9 (5.5mm) needles, cast on 54(60) sts in A, marking 18th and 37th(43rd) st with a stitch marker or small safety pin.

Work 14(16) rows in st st beg with a k row.

Larger size only

Next row: K4, [ssk, k8] 3 times, [k2tog, k8] twice, k2tog, k4. *(54 sts)*

Next row: Purl.

Both sizes

Next row: K3, [sl2, k1, p2sso, k6] 5 times, sl2, k1, p2sso, k3. *(42 sts)*

Next and every WS row unless stated otherwise: Purl.
Next RS row: K2, [sl2, k1, p2sso, k4] 5 times, sl2, k1, p2sso, k2. *(30 sts)*
Next RS row: K1, [sl2, k1, p2sso, k2] 5 times, sl2, k1, p2sso, k1. *(18 sts)*
Next row (WS): [P2tog] to end. *(9 sts)*
Break yarn leaving a long tail. Thread yarn tail through rem sts, pull up tightly, and secure.
Turn piece so cast-on edge is uppermost.
Pick up and knit 18 sts from second stitch marker or safety pin to outside edge and then cont and pick up and knit 18 sts from second outside edge to first stitch marker or safety pin. *(36 sts)*
Next row: K1, ssk, k to last 3 sts, k2tog, k1. *(34 sts)*
Next row: Purl.
Rep last 2 rows, 10(14) times more. *(14/6 sts)*
Smaller size only
Next row: K1, ssk, k to last 3 sts, k2tog, k1. *(12 sts)*
Next row: P2tog, p to last 2 sts, p2tog tbl. *(10 sts)*
Next row: K1, ssk, k4, k2tog, k1. *(8 sts)*
Next row: P2tog, p4, p2tog tbl. *(6 sts)*
Both sizes
Next row: K1, ssk, k2tog, k1. *(4 sts)*
Next row: P2tog, p2tog tbl. *(2 sts)*
Next row: K2tog. *(1 st)*
Mark rem st with a stitch marker or small safety pin and do not break yarn. With circular needle, cont to pick up and knit 88(94) sts up right side of work, across cast-on edge of hat and down left side of work, stopping at the stitch before the marker. *(89/95 sts)*
Next round: Purl.
Next round: K1, m1, k to st with marker, m1. *(91/97 sts)*

Next round: Purl.
Bind (cast) off kwise.

Spine strip

(Make 1)
*Using US9 (5.5mm) needles and B double, make a slip knot.
Row 1 (RS): Inc. *(2 sts)*
Row 2: Inc, k1. *(3 sts)*
Row 3: Inc, k2. *(4 sts)*
Row 4: Inc, k3. *(5 sts)*
Row 5: Inc, k4. *(6 sts)*
Row 6: Inc, k5. *(7 sts)*
Row 7: Inc, k6. *(8 sts)*
Row 8: Inc, k7. *(9 sts)*
Break yarn and leave sts on spare needle.**
Rep from * to ** 3(4) times more.

FINAL SPINE
Make as for other spines but do not break yarn.
Next row: K across sts on final spine then knit across sts on rem 4(5) spines, making sure the RS of the spine is facing (if you have put them on a standard knitting needle, you will need to turn them around). *(45/54 sts)*
Next row: Knit.
Bind (cast) off.

Eye pieces

(Make 2)
Using US8 (5mm) needles, cast on 16 sts in A.
Work 2 rows in st st beg with a k row.
Row 3: [K2tog] to end. *(8 sts)*
Row 4: [P2tog] to end. *(4 sts)*
Break yarn, thread yarn tail through rem sts, pull up tightly, and secure.

Teeth

(Make 1)
Using US8 (5mm) needles, cast on 3 sts in C.
[Bind/cast off 2 sts, slip rem st from RH to LH needle, cast on 2 sts] 9(11) times.
Bind (cast) off.

To make up

Sew seam of eye pieces, leaving cast-on edge open.
Using D, work a coil of chain stitch (see page 124) for eye center on eye pieces. Using a separated strand of C, work a circle of chain stitch around the eye center. Stuff eye piece lightly and sew in place using the photograph as a guide, so that lower edges curls inward.
Sew back seam of hat using flat stitch (see page 126).
Attach spine strip to hat, sewing along both sides of the strip, beginning at the crown and running down the back seam and then the center of the flap.
Sew teeth in place.
Weave in all loose ends.

tortoise booties

Who doesn't love tortoises with their slow and gentle approach to life? Admittedly, the baby in your life may not have quite the same attitude, but you can always hope! And, at the very least, you can be sure that the colorful yarn I've used for these booties is guaranteed to keep tiny toes warm when the temperature dips.

YARN AND MATERIALS

Lion Brand Wool-Ease Tonal (80% acrylic, 20% wool), 124yd (113m) per 4oz (113g) ball of bulky (chunky) yarn

    1 ball in Fern 171 (A)

Oddment of bulky (chunky) yarn in beige (B)

Oddment of light worsted (DK) yarn in black (C)

NEEDLES AND EQUIPMENT

Pair of US8 (5mm) knitting needles

Yarn sewing needle

Large-eyed embroidery needle

SIZE

To fit an average baby 0–6 (6–12) months

(For more information on sizes, see page 112)

Actual measurements: approx. length 3½in/8.25cm (4in/10cm)

GAUGE (TENSION)

16 sts and 20 rows to 4in (10cm) square over stockinette (stocking) stitch on US8 (5mm) needles

ABBREVIATIONS

See page 127

Main bootie

(Make 2)

Cast on 22(24) sts.

Work 6 rows in st st beg with a k row.

Row 7: K7(8), [k1, p1] twice, m1, [p1, k1] twice, turn.

Row 8: K1, [p1, k1] 4 times, turn.

Work on 9 sts just worked, leaving rem sts on needles.

Row 9: K1, [p1, k1] to end.

Rep row 9, 5(7) times more.

Leave sts on needle and break yarn.

With RS facing, rejoin yarn to right-hand edge at base of rectangle just worked.

Using A, pick up and knit 5(6) sts up first side and k2 on needle, using B, k5 sts on needle; using A from center of ball, k rem sts on needle, pick up and knit 5(6) sts down second side and k rem 7(8) sts. *(33/37 sts)*

Next row: In A, p14(16); in B, p5; in A, p to end.

Work 2 rows in st st, beg with a k row, keeping to the color patt.

Break B and A from center of ball, and work rem of bootie in A.

Next row: K3, k2tog, k to last 5 sts, ssk, k3. *(31/35 sts)*

Next row: Knit.

Rep last 2 rows once more. *(29/33 sts)*

Next row: K3, k2tog, k6(7), ssk, k3(5), k2tog, k6(7), ssk, k3. *(25/29 sts)*

Next row: Knit.

Next row: K3, k2tog, k4(5), ssk, k3(5), k2tog, k4(5), ssk, k3. *(21/25 sts)*

Bind (cast) off kwise.

Legs

(Make 8)

Cast on 4 sts in B.

Row 1: Knit.

Row 2: Purl.

Break yarn and thread through rem sts.

To make up

Sew back and sole seam using flat stitch (see page 126).
Using C, work two French knots (see page 124) for the
tortoise's eyes.
Using the same yarn, work two straight stitches (see page
124) in a flattened V shape for the mouth.
To define the head, run a length of B around the entire
outside of the head section worked in B, pull slightly into a
rounded shape, and secure.
Seam the cast-on and bound- (cast-) off edges of the legs
and stitch in place.
Weave in all loose ends.

monster feet

These feet are sure to please the little monsters in your life. I've made them in a foot-friendly and washable acrylic, perfect for small children, and because they're worked in a super-thick yarn and knitted flat, they're one of the easiest projects in the book. You may even find yourself getting addicted and knitting them to match a whole range of outfits!

YARN AND MATERIALS

Lion Brand Hometown USA (100% acrylic), 81yd (74m) per 5oz (142g) ball of super bulky (super chunky) yarn

1 ball in Key Lime 171 (A)

Oddment of bulky (chunky) yarn in off-white (B)

NEEDLES AND EQUIPMENT

Pair of US10½ (6.5mm) knitting needles

Yarn sewing needle

Small nylon brush, such as a toothbrush (optional)

SIZE

To fit a child 2–3 (4–6) years

(For more information on sizes, see page 112)

Actual measurements: approx. 5in/12.5cm (5¾in/14.5cm) from toe to heel (unstretched, and not including monster toes)

GAUGE (TENSION)

10 sts and 16 rows to 4in (10cm) square over stockinette (stocking) stitch on US10½ (6.5mm) needles using A.

ABBREVIATIONS

See page 127

Main slipper sock

(Make 2)
Cast on 22(24) sts in A.
Work 6 rows in st st beg with a k row.
Row 7: K15(16), turn.
Row 8: P7(8), turn.
Row 9: Sl1 pwise WYB, k to end.
Row 10: Sl1 pwise, p to end.
Rep rows 9–10, twice (3 times) more.
Leave sts on needle and break yarn.
With RS facing, rejoin yarn to right-hand edge at base of rectangle just worked.
Pick up and knit 5(6) sts up first side, k8 sts on needle, pick up and knit 5(6) sts down second side, k rem 7(8) sts. *(32/36 sts)*
Work 3 rows in st st beg with a p row.
Next row: K3, k2tog, k to last 5 sts, ssk, k3. *(30/34 sts)*
Next row: Knit.
Rep last 2 rows once more. *(28/32 sts)*
Next row: K3, k2tog, k5(7), ssk, k4, k2tog, k5(7), ssk, k3. *(24/28 sts)*
Next row: Knit.
Next row: K3, k2tog, k3(5), ssk, k4, k2tog, k3(5), ssk, k3. *(20/24 sts)*
Bind (cast) off kwise.

Toes

(Make 6)
Using A, cast on 6 sts.
Knit 2 rows.
Break A and join in B, using it double.
Work 2 rows in st st beg with a k row.
Row 5: [K2tog] 3 times. *(3 sts)*
Break yarn and thread through rem sts.

To make up

Sew back and sole seam using flat stitch (see page 126).
Join seams on toes, leaving cast-on edge open for stuffing. Stuff toes lightly with some spare yarn and sew in place using the photograph as a guide.
Weave in all loose ends.
Dampen slippers and using nylon brush, gently brush finished slipper socks around the toes to give them a fluffy look.

raccoon hat

The cheeky raccoon makes the perfect hat character for your own cute little one. And I love this 100 percent wool, super-soft luxury yarn, which comes in great raccoon shades. This hat makes a great first project for people who want to try their hand at knitting with more than one color at once, without embarking on anything too intricate.

YARN AND MATERIALS

Sugar Bush Yarns Crisp (100% wool), 95yd (87m) per 1¾oz (50g) ball of light worsted (DK) yarn

    1 ball in Snowbird 2001 (A)

    1(2) ball(s) in Titanium 2018 (B)

    1 ball in Lead 2019 (C)

Oddment of light worsted (DK) yarn in black (D)

2 x ⁹⁄₁₆in (14mm) shiny black shank buttons

NEEDLES AND EQUIPMENT

Pair of US5 (3.75mm) knitting needles

Yarn sewing needle

Large-eyed embroidery needle

Nylon brush, such as a toothbrush (optional)

SIZE

To fit baby 3–6 (6–12) months

(For more information on sizes, see page 112)

Actual measurements: approx. 12¾in/ 32.5cm (15in/38cm) circumference (unstretched)

GAUGE (TENSION)

22 sts and 28 rows to 4in (10cm) square over stockinette (stocking) stitch on US5 (3.75mm needles)

ABBREVIATIONS

See page 127

Main hat

LOWER FRONT

(Make 1)

Using US5 (3.75mm) needles, cast on 36(42) sts in A.
Knit 4 rows.
Break A and join in B.
Work next 16 rows from chart (overleaf), ending with a WS row.
Work 10(16) rows in st st beg with a k row.
Break yarn and leave sts on a spare needle.

LOWER BACK

(Make 1)

Using US5 (3.75mm) needles, cast on 36(42) sts in A.
Knit 4 rows.
Break A and join in B.
Work 26(32) rows in st st beg with a k row.
To complete hat, work 36(42) sts from lower back followed by 36(42) sts from lower front (on spare needle) as follows:

Larger size only

Next row: [K5, k2tog] to end. *(72 sts)*
Next row: Purl.

Both sizes

Next row: [K4, k2tog] to end. *(60 sts)*
Next and every foll WS row unless stated otherwise: Purl.
Next RS row: [K3, k2tog] to end. *(48 sts)*
Next RS row: [K2, k2tog] to end. *(36 sts)*
Next RS row: [K1, k2tog] to end. *(24 sts)*
Next RS row: [K2tog] to end. *(12 sts)*
Next row: [P2tog] to end. *(6 sts)*
Break yarn and thread through rem sts.

Ear

(Make 4)
Cast on 8 sts in B.
Work 4 rows in st st beg with a k row.
Row 5: K1, ssk, k2, k2tog, k1. *(6 sts)*
Row 6: Purl.
Row 7: K1, ssk, k2tog, k1. *(4 sts)*
Row 8: P2tog, p2tog tbl. *(2 sts)*
Row 9: K2tog. *(1 st)*
Fasten off.

To make up

Sew side seam from top of crown to base on one side of hat and from bottom of crown to base on the other.
Seam ear pieces together along sides and bottom.
Stitch in place along front and back, using the photograph as a guide.
Sew buttons in place for eyes.
Using D, work a small coil of chain stich (see page 124) for nose.
Weave in all loose ends.
Dampen ears and brush with small nylon brush to give a fluffy look.

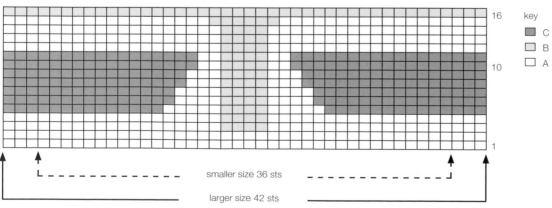

16

10

1

key

■ C
■ B
□ A

smaller size 36 sts

larger size 42 sts

pocket buddy socks

These cute socks for tiny feet are a great basic pattern for pre-schoolers. I've knitted mine in a subtle turquoise, but there are lots of other great shades to choose from. And the yarn is 100 percent wool, but also washable. Best of all, I've added a little pocket where the owner can stash secret treasures—or one or even two of these little knitted rabbits: you never know when you're going to need a special friend.

SKILL LEVEL

YARN AND MATERIALS
Plymouth Select DK Merino (100% wool), 130yd (119m) per 1¾oz (50g) ball of light worsted (DK) yarn

    2 balls in 1131 (A)

Oddments of one or two light worsted (DK) yarns in colors of your choice (B)

Oddment of light worsted (DK) yarn in dark gray (C)

Handful of polyester toy filing

NEEDLES AND EQUIPMENT
Set of 4 US6 (4mm) double-pointed knitting needles

Set of 4 US5 (3.75mm) double-pointed knitting needles

Pair of US3 (3.25mm) knitting needles

Stitch holder (optional)

Yarn sewing needle

Large-eyed embroidery needle

SIZE
To fit a child 2–4 (4–6) years

(For more information on sizes, see page 112)

Actual measurements: approx. 6in/15cm (7¼in/18.5cm) from toe to heel (unstretched)

GAUGE (TENSION)
22 sts and 28 rows to 4in (10cm) square over stockinette (stocking) stitch on US5 (3.75mm) needles

ABBREVIATIONS
See page 127

Main sock
(Make 2)
Using set of US6 (4mm) needles, cast on 40(44) sts in A.
Round 1: Knit.
Round 2: Purl.
Rep rounds 1–2 once more.
Change to set of US5 (3.75mm) needles.
Smaller size only
Knit 32 rounds, on the last round running a thread through sts 7–18 inclusive on first sock and sts 23–34 inclusive on second sock (you will use these to form pockets).
Knit 18 rounds.

Larger size only
Knit 36 rounds, on the last round running a thread through sts 8–19 inclusive on first sock and sts 26–37 inclusive on second sock (you will use these to form pockets).
Knit 22 rounds.

HEEL

Both sizes
K10(11), turn.
Next row: P20(22), turn.
Work rem of heel on 20(22) sts just worked, leaving rem 20(22) sts for instep on stitch holder or spare needle.
Next row: Sl1 pwise, k to end.
Next row: Sl1 pwise, p to end.
Rep last 2 rows 4(5) times more.
Next row: K12(13), ssk, k1, turn. *(19/21 sts)*
Next row: Sl1 pwise, p5, p2tog, p1, turn. *(18/20 sts)*
Next row: Sl1 pwise, k to 1 st before gap, ssk, k1, turn. *(17/19 sts)*
Next row: Sl1 pwise, p to 1 st before gap, p2tog, p1, turn. *(16/18 sts)*
Rep last 2 rows once (twice) more. *(14 sts)*
Next row: Sl1 pwise, k to st before gap, ssk, turn.
Next row: Sl1 pwise, p to last 2 sts, p2tog. *(12 sts)*

HEEL GUSSET

On needle 1: Using B, k across all heel sts and pick up and knit 7(8) sts up side of heel flap.
On needle 2: K all 20(22) instep sts.
On needle 3: Pick up and knit 7(8) sts up side of heel flap and k6 of heel sts. *(46/50 sts)*
Put marker on next st to mark beg of round.
Next round: On needle 1, k to last 3 sts, k2tog, k1; on needle 2, k all sts; on needle 3, k1, ssk, k to end. *(44/48 sts)*
Next round: Knit.
Rep last 2 rounds 4 times more. *(36/40 sts)*

FOOT

Knit 10(16) rounds.

TOE

Round 1: On needle 1, k to last 3 sts, k2tog, k1; on needle 2, k1, ssk, k to last 3 sts, k2tog, k1; on needle 3, k1, ssk, k to end. *(32/36 sts)*
Round 2: Knit.
Rep rounds 1–2 once more. *(28/32 sts)*
Round 5: On needle 1, k to last 3 sts, k2tog, k1; on needle 2, k1, ssk, k to last 3 sts, k2tog, k1; on needle 3, k1, ssk, k to end. *(24/28 sts)*
Rep round 5, 4(5) times more. *(8 sts)*
Break yarn, thread through rem sts, and secure.

Pockets

With RS facing, run a standard US5 (3.75mm) knitting needle through a path of thread from left to right.
Work 11 rows in st st beg with a k row.
Row 12: Knit.
Bind (cast) off.
Rep with each path of thread.

To make up

Create pockets by sewing down sides.
Weave in all loose ends.

Rabbit

HEAD AND BODY
(Make 2)
Using US3 (3.25mm) needles, cast on 6 sts in B.
Work 6 rows in st st beg with a k row.
Row 7: K1, ssk, k2tog, k1. *(4 sts)*
Row 8: Purl.
Row 9: [Inc] to end. *(8 sts)*
Work 5 rows in st st beg with a p row.
Row 15: K2, bind (cast) off 4 sts, k to end. *(2 groups of 2 sts)*
Work on last 2 sts worked only, leaving rem 2 sts on needle.
*Work 4 rows in st st beg with a p row.
Next row: P2tog. *(1 st)*
Fasten off.**
Rejoin yarn to rem 2 sts on WS of work.
Rep from * to **.

Legs

(Make 2)
Cast on 10 sts in B.
Row 1: K3, ssk, k2tog, k3. *(8 sts)*
Row 2: P2, p2tog, p2tog tbl, p2. *(6 sts)*
Row 3: K1, ssk, k2tog, k1. *(4 sts)*
Work 5 rows in st st beg with a p row.
Bind (cast) off.

Arms

(Make 2)
Cast on 4 sts in B.
Work 6 rows in st st beg with a k row.
Row 7: K1, k2tog, k1. *(3 sts)*
Break yarn, thread through rem sts, and secure.

To make up

Seam head and body piece, leaving lower edge open. Stuff piece and close lower edge. Seam arms without stuffing. Seam legs, stuffing feet and lightly stuffing main leg as you go. Stitch limbs in place.
Using C, work two French knots (see page 124) for eyes and a cross for the nose and mouth.
Weave in all loose ends.

CHAPTER 2

in-betweeners

unicorn hat

Pretty, magical, and rainbow cool, unicorns are a bit like horses, only better. So it's no wonder that over the past few years, unicorns have captured the imagination of little (and not-so-little) girls with big dreams and ambitions. I've decorated the horn on this hat with a little knitted flower, but if you prefer, you could choose sew-on gems or even ribbons to make your unicorn one of a kind.

YARN AND MATERIALS

Cascade Pacific Chunky (60% acrylic, 40% wool), 120yd (110m) per 3½oz (100g) ball of bulky (chunky) yarn

   1 ball in Baby Pink 06 (A)

   1 ball in Blue Mist 92 (B)

Oddment of bulky (chunky) yarn in white (C)

Oddment of light worsted (DK) yarn in dark gray (D)

Oddment of bulky (chunky) yarn in bright pink (E)

A medium white button

Handful of polyester toy filling

NEEDLES AND EQUIPMENT

Pair of US9 (5.5mm) knitting needles

4 x stitch markers or small safety pins

US M-13 (9mm) crochet hook or one of similar size

Pompom maker to make 1¾in (4.5cm) pompoms, or four cardboard circles each measuring 1¾in (4.5cm) in diameter with a ¾-in (18-mm) hole in the center

Yarn sewing needle

Large-eyed embroidery needle

SIZE

To fit a child 7–9 (10–12) years

(For more information on sizes, see page 112)

Actual measurements: approx. 18½in/47cm (20in/51cm) circumference (unstretched)

GAUGE (TENSION)

14 sts and 20 rows to 4in (10cm) square over stockinette (stocking) stitch on US9 (5.5mm) needles

ABBREVIATIONS

See page 127

Main hat

(Make 1)

Cast on 66(72) sts in A, marking 12th, 23rd, 44th, and 55th sts (14th, 25th, 48th, and 59th sts).

Knit 4 rows.

Work 20(22) rows in st st beg with a k row.

Larger size only

Next row: K5, [k2tog, k10] 5 times, k2tog, k5. *(66 sts)*

Next row: Purl.

Both sizes

Next row: K4, [sl2, k1, p2sso, k8] 5 times, sl2, k1, p2sso, k4. *(54 sts)*

Next and every WS row unless stated otherwise: Purl.

Next RS row: K3, [sl2, k1, p2sso, k6] 5 times, sl2, k1, p2sso, k3. *(42 sts)*

Next RS row: K2, [sl2, k1, p2sso, k4] 5 times, sl2, k1, p2sso, k2. *(30 sts)*

Next RS row: K1, [sl2, k1, p2sso, k2] 5 times, sl2, k1, p2sso, k1. *(18 sts)*

Next RS row: [Sl2, k1, p2sso] to end. *(6 sts)*

Break yarn leaving a long tail. Thread yarn tail through rem sts, pull up tightly, and secure.

Ear flaps

With RS facing, pick up and knit 12 sts between first two markers on cast-on edge.

Knit 3 rows.

Row 4: K1, ssk, k to last 3 sts, k2tog, k1. *(10 sts)*

Row 5: Knit.

Rep rows 4–5 twice more. *(6 sts)*

Row 10: K1, ssk, k2tog, k1. *(4 sts)*

Row 11: Knit.

Row 12: Ssk, k2tog. *(2 sts)*

Row 13: K2tog. *(1 st)*

Fasten off.

Rep between second two markers to make second ear flap.

Ear

(Make 4)

Cast on 8 sts in A.

Work 6 rows in st st beg with a k row.

Row 7: K1, ssk, k2, k2tog, k1. *(6 sts)*

Row 8: Purl.

Row 9: K1, ssk, k2tog, k1. *(4 sts)*

Row 10: P2tog, p2tog tbl. *(2 sts)*

Row 11: K2tog. *(1 st)*

Fasten off.

Horn

(Make 1)

Cast on 12 sts in C.

Work 2 rows in st st beg with a k row.

Row 3: K1, k2tog, k to last 3 sts, ssk, k1. *(10 sts)*

Work 3 rows in st st beg with a p row.

Rep rows 3–6 (last 4 rows) twice more. *(6 sts)*

Row 15: K1, k2tog, ssk, k1. *(4 sts)*

Row 16: P2tog, p2tog tbl. *(2 sts)*

Row 17: K2tog. *(1 st)*

Fasten off.

Mane

(Make 1)

Using the crochet hook and B double, make a 2-yd (2-m) crochet chain (see page 123).

Flower

(Make 1)

Using E, cast on 4 sts.

*Row 1: Inc, k to end. *(5 sts)*

Row 2: Purl.

Row 3: Skpo, bind (cast) off 3 sts. *(1 st)*

Pass rem st from RH to LH needle.**

Cast on 3 sts. *(4 sts)*

Rep from * to ** 3 times.

Cast on 3 sts. *(4 sts)*

Row 1: Inc, k to end. *(5 sts)*

Row 2: Purl.

Row 3: Skpo, bind (cast) off 3 sts. *(1 st)*

Fasten off.

To make up

Sew the long seam of the horn and stuff, fairly lightly. Using B, work a spiral of chain stitch (see page 124) around and up the horn.

Sew ear pieces together then sew the ears in place, using the photograph as a guide.

Sew horn in between ears.

Using D, work the eyes in chain stitch.

Stitch the mane in place from just behind the horn to the base of the hat, by forming the chain into a series of loops, each about 1½in (4cm) high, and stitching it in place as you go.

Gather along lower edge of flower pieces and stitch into a circle. Stitch flower in place and sew button in center using a separated length of B.

Using the crochet hook and A double, make two 3-in (8-cm) crochet chains. Using pompom maker or cardboard circles and B, make two pompoms. Using yarn tails on crochet chains, sew one end to the pompoms and the other end to the bottom of the earflaps.

Weave in all loose ends.

fox socks

With their colorful coats and bushy tails, foxes are one of the most photogenic of all wild animals, and they're also the most common wild carnivores worldwide. Fox socks, on the other hand, are still quite rare. But you can now change all that by whipping up a pair for the fox fanatic in your life. Go red, like I have here, or opt for shades of icy white and gray and create your own Arctic fox versions.

SKILL LEVEL

YARN AND MATERIALS

Debbie Bliss Baby Cashmerino (53% wool, 33% acrylic, 12% cashmere), 137yd (125m) per 1¾oz (50g) ball of light worsted (DK) yarn

> 2 balls in Sienna 067 (A)
> 1 ball in White 100 (B)

Oddment of light worsted (DK) yarn in black (C)

NEEDLES AND EQUIPMENT

Set of US3 (3.25mm) double-pointed knitting needles

Pair of US3 (3.25mm) knitting needles

Stitch holder or large safety pin

Yarn sewing needle

Large-eyed embroidery needle

SIZE

To fit a child 7–9 (10–12) years

(For more information on sizes, see page 112)

Actual measurements: approx. 7in/18cm (8in/20cm) from toe to heel (unstretched)

GAUGE (TENSION)

24 sts and 32 rows to 4in (10cm) square over stockinette (stocking) stitch on US3 (3.25mm) needles

ABBREVIATIONS

See page 127

Main sock

(Make 2)
Using set of needles, cast on 44(48) sts in A.
Work 13 rounds in k2, p2 rib.
Knit 49(55) rounds.

HEEL
Next round: K11(12), turn.
Next row: P22(24).
Work rem of heel on 22(24) sts just worked, leaving rem 22(24) sts for instep on stitch holder or spare needle.
Next row: Sl1 pwise, k to end.
Next row: Sl1 pwise, p to end.
Rep last 2 rows 6(7) times more.
Next row: K13(14), ssk, k1, turn. *(21/23 sts)*
Next row: Sl1 pwise, p5, p2tog, p1, turn. *(20/22 sts)*
Next row: Sl1 pwise, k to 1 st before gap, ssk, k1, turn. *(19/21 sts)*
Next row: Sl1 pwise, p to 1 st before gap, p2tog, p1, turn. *(18/20 sts)*
Rep last 2 rows twice more. *(14/16 sts)*

Larger size only
Next row: Sl1 pwise, k to st before gap, ssk, turn. *(15 sts)*
Next row: Sl1 pwise, p to last 2 sts, p2tog. *(14 sts)*

Both sizes
HEEL GUSSET
On needle 1: K across all heel sts and pick up and knit 9(10) sts up side of heel flap.
On needle 2: K across all 22(24) instep sts.
On needle 3: Pick up and knit 9(10) sts up side of heel flap and k 7 sts across heel. *(54/58 sts)*
Put marker on next st to mark beg of round.
Next round: On needle 1, k to last 3 sts, k2tog; on needle 2, k across all sts; on needle 3, k1, ssk, k to end. *(52/56 sts)*
Next round: Knit.
Rep last 2 rounds 6 times more. *(40/44 sts)*
Knit 10(14) rounds.
Break A.

Break yarn and leave rem sts on stitch holder or safety pin..
With RS facing, rejoin B to rem 18(20) sts on underside
of sock.
Work 10 rows in st st beg with a k row.
Row 11: K1, ssk, k to last 3 sts, k2tog, k1. *(16/18 sts)*
Row 12: Purl.
Row 13: K1, ssk, k to last 3 sts, k2tog, k1. *(14/16 sts)*
Row 14: P1, p2tog, p to last 3 sts, p2tog tbl, p1.
(12/14 sts)
Rep rows 13–14 twice more. *(4/6 sts)*
Larger size only
Row 19: K1, ssk, k to last 3 sts, k2tog, k1. *(4 sts)*
Both sizes
Put rem sts on a stitch holder or safety pin.

Ear

(Make 8)
Cast on 6 sts in A.
Work 4 rows in st st beg with a k row.
Row 5: Ssk, k2, k2tog. *(4 sts)*
Row 6: Purl.
Row 7: Ssk, k2tog. *(2 sts)*
Row 8: P2tog. *(1 st)*
Fasten off.

To make up

Thread yarn tail through all stitches at toe end of sock, pull
tightly, and secure.
Seam the side seams of the foot part of the socks using
flat stitch (see page 126).
Using C, embroider a flattened U-shape for the eyes using
chain stitch (see page 124). Using C, work a coil of chain
stitch for the nose.
For the ears, pair up pieces, seam the sides, and sew in
place using the photograph as a guide.
Weave in all loose ends.

For top of sock, work on 22(24) instep sts on needle 2,
leaving rem sts on stitch holder or spare needle.
Row 1: K3(4) in B, 16 in A, 3(4) in B, using yarn from
ball center.
Row 2: P3(4) in B, 16 in A, 3(4) in B.
Row 3: K4(5) in B, 14 in A, 4(5) in B.
Row 4: P4(5) in B, 14 in A, 4(5) in B.
Row 5: K5(6) in B, 12 in A, 5(6) in B.
Row 6: P5(6) in B, 12 in A, 5(6) in B.
Row 7: K6(7) in B, 10 in A, 6(7) in B.
Row 8: P6(7) in B, 10 in A, 6(7) in B.
Row 9: K7(8) in B, 8 in A, 7(8) in B.
Row 10: P7(8) in B, 8 in A, 7(8) in B.
Row 11: K1, ssk, k5(6) in B, k6 in A, k5(6), k2tog, k1 in B.
(20/22 sts)
Row 12: P7(8) in B, 6 in A, 7(8) in B.
Row 13: K1, ssk, k5(6) in B, k4 in A, k5(6), k2tog, k1 in B.
(18/20 sts)
Row 14: P1, p2tog, p4(5) in B, p4 in A, p4(5), p2tog tbl,
p1 in B. *(16/18 sts)*
Row 15: K1, ssk, k4(5) in B, k2 in A, k4(5), k2tog, k1 in B.
(14/16 sts)
Row 16: P1, p2tog, p3(4) in B, p2 in A, p3(4), p2tog tbl,
p1 in B. *(12/14 sts)*
Row 17: K1, ssk, k2(3) in B, k2 in A, k2(3), k2tog, k1 in B.
(10/12 sts)
Row 18: P1, p2tog, p1(2) in B, p2 in A, p1(2), p2tog tbl,
p1 in B. *(8/10 sts)*
Larger size only
Row 19: K1, ssk, k1 in B, k2 in A, k1, k2tog, k1 in B.
(8 sts)

whale socks

It's hard to get your head around a blue whale—the largest animal to have ever lived and who has a heart the size of a car. So you'll be pleased to hear that these whale socks are a whole lot easier to understand. They're knitted in my favorite shade of blue and are just the thing to slip on small feet when a chill wind blows. And don't forget to look out for the cute whale tail; if that doesn't win you over, nothing will.

YARN AND MATERIALS
Cascade 128 Superwash (100% wool), 128yd (117m) per 3½oz (100g) ball of bulky (chunky) yarn

    1 ball in Denim 845 (A)

Oddment of light worsted (DK) in black (B)

Oddment of light worsted (DK) in off-white (C)

NEEDLES AND EQUIPMENT
Pair of US10½ (6.5mm) knitting needles

Pair of US9 (5.5mm) knitting needles

2 x stitch holders

Yarn sewing needle

Large-eyed embroidery needle

SIZE
To fit a child 7–9 (10–12) years

(For more information on sizes, see page 112)

Actual measurements: approx. 7¾in/19.5cm (8½in/21.5cm) from toe to heel (unstretched)

GAUGE (TENSION)
14 sts and 20 rows to 4in (10cm) square over stockinette (stocking) stitch on US9 (5.5mm) needles

ABBREVIATIONS
See page 127

Main sock
(Make 2)
Using US10½ (6.5mm) needles, cast on 28(32) sts in A.
Change to US9 (5.5mm) needles.
Work 10(12) rows in st st beg with a k row.

HEEL
Slip first 7(8) sts onto stitch holder 1, slip next 14(16) sts onto stitch holder 2.
With RS facing and US9 (5.5mm) needles, rejoin yarn to inner edge of 7(8) sts at end of row and knit to end, turn first stitch holder around and k7(8) sts. *(14/16 sts)*
Work on 14(16) sts just knitted, leaving instep sts on second stitch holder.

Work 9(11) rows in st st beg with a p row.
Next row: K8(9), ssk, k1, turn.
Next row: P4, p2tog, p1, turn.
Next row: K5, ssk, k1, turn.
Next row: P6, p2tog, p1, turn.
Larger size only
Next row: K7, ssk, k1, turn.
Next row: P8, p2tog, p1, turn.
Both sizes
Next row: K to last 2 sts, ssk.
Next row: P to last 2 sts, p2tog. *(8 sts)*

HEEL GUSSET
With RS facing and US9 (5.5mm) needles, rejoin yarn to right-hand side of heel flap and pick up and knit 7(8) sts up one side of heel, k across 8 sts of heel, and pick up and knit 7(8) sts down other side of heel. *(22/24 sts)*
Next row: Purl.
Next row: K1, ssk, k to last 3 sts, k2tog, k1. *(20/22 sts)*
Work 3 rows in st st beg with a p row.
Rep last 4 rows twice more. *(16/18 sts)*
Next row: K1, ssk, k to last 3 sts, k2tog, k1. *(14/16 sts)*

FOOT
Work 11(15) rows in st st beg with a p row.

TOE
*Next row: K1, ssk, k to last 3 sts, k2tog, k1. *(12/14 sts)*
Next row: P1, p2tog, p to last 2 sts, p2tog tbl, p1. *(10/12 sts)*
Rep last 2 rows once more. *(6/8 sts)*
Leave sts on stitch holder or spare needle.**

BASE OF FOOT
Turn stitch holder with sts around and with RS facing, work 24(28) rows in st st beg with a k row.
Rep from * to **.

Fin A

(Make 4)
Using US9 (5.5mm) needles and A, cast on 5 sts.
Work 2 rows in st st beg with a k row.
Row 3: Ssk, k2, m1, k1.
Row 4: Purl.
Bind (cast) off.

Fin B

(Make 4)
Using US9 (5.5mm) needles and A, cast on 5 sts.
Work 2 rows in st st beg with a k row.
Row 3: K1, m1, k2, k2tog.
Row 4: Purl.
Bind (cast) off.

Tail

(Make 4)
Using US9 (5.5mm) needles and A, cast on 6 sts.
Work 4 rows in st st beg with a k row.
Row 5: K1, m1, k2, turn.
Work on 4 sts just worked, leaving rem sts on needle.
Next and every WS row unless stated otherwise: Purl.
Next RS row: K1, m1, k3. *(5 sts)*
Next RS row: K1, m1, k2, k2tog.
Next RS row: Ssk, k1, k2tog. *(3 sts)*
Next row: Bind (cast) off pwise.
Fasten off and rejoin yarn to rem sts on RS of work.
Next row: K2, m1, k1. *(4 sts)*
Next and every WS row unless stated otherwise: Purl.
Next RS row: K3, m1, k1. *(5 sts)*
Next RS row: Ssk, k2, m1, k1.
Next RS row: Ssk, k1, k2tog. *(3 sts)*
Bind (cast) off pwise.

To make up

Graft stitches using Kitchener stitch (see page 125) from both needles to join toe edge.
Join ankle and foot seams of main socks.
Place one fin A piece and one fin B piece together, with the right sides facing outward. Sew around the sides and bound- (cast-) off edges of the piece, then sew the cast-on edges together. Sew the fins in place along their cast-on edges, using the photograph as a guide.
Place two tail pieces together, with the right sides facing outward. Sew around the curved edges, leaving the cast-on edges open. Sew the tail in place on the heel along both the upper and lower cast-on edges.
Using B, work French knots (see page 124) for the eye centers. Using C, work a circle of chain stitch (see page 124) around each French knot.
Using B, work a curved line in chain stitch for the mouth.
Weave in all loose ends.

lion hat

Who can resist majestic male lions with their shaggy manes and roars that can be heard up to five miles away? Knitted in a thick yarn in a gorgeous golden shade, this hat is guaranteed to keep your own little king or queen of the jungle super-warm. And once you've got the hang of it, the loopy stitch I've used for the mane is very quick to knit.

YARN AND MATERIALS
Cascade 128 Superwash (100% wool), 128yd (117m) per 3½oz (100g) ball of bulky (chunky) yarn

    1 ball in Daffodil 821 (A)

Lion Brand Wool-Ease Thick & Quick (80% acrylic, 20% wool), 106yd (97m) per 6oz (170g) ball of super bulky (super chunky) yarn

    1 ball in Butterscotch 189 (B)

Oddment of light worsted (DK) yarn in black (C)

NEEDLES AND EQUIPMENT
Pair of US9 (5.5mm) knitting needles

Pair of US11 (8mm) knitting needles

US I-9 (5.5mm) crochet hook or one of similar size

4 x stitch markers or small safety pins

Yarn sewing needle

Large-eyed embroidery needle

SIZE
To fit a child 7–9 (10–12) years

(For more information on sizes, see page 112)

Actual measurements: approx. 17½in/44cm (18¾in/48cm) circumference (unstretched)

GAUGE (TENSION)
15 sts and 22 rows to 4in (10cm) square over stockinette (stocking) stitch on US9 (5.5mm) needles

ABBREVIATIONS
See page 127

Main hat
(Make 1)

Using US9 (5.5mm) needles, cast on 66(72) sts in A, marking 12th, 23rd, 44th, and 55th sts (14th, 25th, 48th, and 59th sts) with stitch markers or small safety pins. Work 24 (26) rows in st st beg with a k row.

Larger size only

Next row: K5, [k2tog, k10] 5 times, k2tog, k5. *(66 sts)*
Next row: Purl.

Both sizes

Next row: K4, [sl2, k1, p2sso, k8] 5 times, sl2, k1, p2sso, k4. *(54 sts)*
Next and every WS row unless stated otherwise: Purl.
Next RS row: K3, [sl2, k1, p2sso, k6] 5 times, sl2, k1, p2sso, k3. *(42 sts)*

Ear

(Make 2)
Using US9 (5.5mm) needles, cast on 8 sts in A.
Work 4 rows in st st beg with a k row.
Row 5: K1, ssk, k2, k2tog, k1. *(6 sts)*
Row 6: Purl.
Row 7: K1, ssk, k2tog, k1. *(4 sts)*
Row 8: Purl.
Row 9: K1, m1, k to last st, m1, k1. *(6 sts)*
Row 10: Purl.
Rep rows 9–10 once more. *(8 sts)*
Work 2 rows in st st beg with a k row.
Bind (cast) off.

Mane

(Make 1)
Using US11 (8mm) needles, cast on 52(58) sts in B.
Make loops in every st as follows:
Knit next st but do not take it off left-hand needle. Bring yarn forward between needles, around thumb of left hand and then back between needles. Knit into back of "old" st still on left-hand needle. Pass first stitch knitted over the stitch just worked (see page 124).
Bind (cast) off.

To make up

Join back seam of hat using flat stitch (see page 126). Stitch the mane in place around the head, beginning and ending at the tip of the ear flaps. The mane should run just behind the ears and about ¾in (2cm) to the front of the very top of hat.
Fold ear pieces in half with the right sides facing outward and seam around curved and lower edges. Stitch ears in place using the photograph as a guide.
Using C, work a curved row of chain stitch (see page 124) for the eyes. Use the same yarn to work a coil of chain stitch for the nose and add a short straight line of chain stitch just below it, again using the photograph as a guide. Weave in all loose ends.

Next RS row: K2, [sl2, k1, p2sso, k4] 5 times, sl2, k1, p2sso, k2. *(30 sts)*
Next RS row: K1, [sl2, k1, p2sso, k2] 5 times, sl2, k1, p2sso, k1. *(18 sts)*
Next row (WS): [P2tog] to end. *(9 sts)*
Break yarn leaving a long tail. Thread yarn tail through rem sts, pull up tightly, and secure.

Ear flaps

With RS facing and using US9 (5.5mm) needles and A, pick up and knit 12 sts between first two markers on cast-on edge.
Work 11 rows in st st beg with a p row.
Row 12: K1, ssk, k to last 3 sts, k2tog, k1. *(10 sts)*
Row 13: Knit.
Rep rows 12–13 twice more. *(6 sts)*
Row 18: K1, ssk, k2tog, k1. *(4 sts)*
Row 19: P2tog, p2tog tbl. *(2 sts)*
Row 20: K2tog. *(1 st)*
Fasten off.
Rep between second two markers to make second ear flap.

little bear hat

This hat is an ideal project for beginners because this little bear has super-easy pompom ears. It's knitted with just one ball of thick yarn, so won't take too long to make, even if you're new to knitting. And the yarn comes in a range of lovely colors. I couldn't resist this soft gray, but if you want something brighter, that would be fabulous too.

YARN AND MATERIALS

Plymouth Yarn Encore Chunky (75% acrylic, 25% wool), 142yd (130m) per 3½oz (100g) ball of bulky (chunky) yarn

  1 ball in 240 (A)

Oddment of light worsted (DK) yarn in black (B)

2 x ½in (12mm) shiny black shank buttons

NEEDLES AND EQUIPMENT

Pair of US9 (5.5mm) knitting needles

Pompom maker to make 1¾in (4.5cm) pompoms, or four cardboard circles each measuring 1¾in (4.5cm) in diameter with a ¾in (18mm) hole in the center

Yarn sewing needle

Large-eyed embroidery needle

SIZE

To fit a child 7–9 (10–12) years

(For more information on sizes, see page 112)

Actual measurements: approx. 18½in/47cm (20in/51cm) circumference (unstretched)

GAUGE (TENSION)

14 sts and 18 rows to 4in (10cm) square over stockinette (stocking) stitch on US9 (5.5mm) needles

ABBREVIATIONS

See page 127

Main hat

(Make 1)
Cast on 66(72) sts in A.
Smaller size only
Row 1: K2, [p2, k2] to end.
Row 2: P2, [k2, p2] to end.
Rep rows 1–2 once more.
Work 18 rows in st st beg with a k row.

Larger size only

Row 1: [K2, p2] to end.

Rep row 1, 3 times more.

Work 22 rows in st st beg with a k row.

Next row: K5, [k2tog, k10] 5 times, k2tog, k5. *(66 sts)*

Next row: Purl.

Both sizes

Next row: K4, [sl2, k1, p2sso, k8] 5 times, sl2, k1, p2sso, k4. *(54 sts)*

Next and every WS row unless stated otherwise: Purl.

Next RS row: K3, [sl2, k1, p2sso, k6] 5 times, sl2, k1, p2sso, k3. *(42 sts)*

Next RS row: K2, [sl2, k1, p2sso, k4] 5 times, sl2, k1, p2sso, k2. *(30 sls)*

Next RS row: K1, [sl2, k1, p2sso, k2] 5 times, sl2, k1, p2sso, k1. *(18 sts)*

Next row (WS): [P2tog] to end. *(9 sts)*

Break yarn leaving a long tail. Thread yarn tail through rem sts, pull up tightly, and secure.

Ear

(Make 2)

Using pompom maker or cardboard circles and A, make two pompoms.

To make up

Join back seam of hat using flat stitch (see page 126). Sew buttons in place for eyes, using the photograph as a guide. Using B, work a coil in chain stitch (see page 124) for the nose and add a vertical straight stitch (see page 124) at the bottom of the nose.

Sew on pompom ears.

Weave in all loose ends.

poodle socks

Did you know that poodles are the official dog of France and were originally bred in Germany as hunting dogs? No? Well, I didn't either. But I do know that with their curly ears and topknots, they're one of the most gorgeous looking canines around. And that's why I wanted to include them here.

SKILL LEVEL

YARN AND MATERIALS

Cascade 220 Superwash (100% wool), 164yd (150m) per 3½oz (100g) ball of worsted (Aran) yarn

    1 ball in Strawberry Cream 894 (A)

    1 ball in Aran 817 (B)

Sirdar Snuggly Snowflake (100% polyester), 67¾yd (62m) per 0.9oz (25g) ball of light worsted (DK) yarn

    1 ball in Creamy 631 (C)

Oddment of light worsted (DK) yarn in black (D)

Very small amount of polyester toy filling

NEEDLES AND EQUIPMENT

Set of 4 US7 (4.5mm) double-pointed knitting needles

Pair of US5 (3.75mm) knitting needles

Stitch holder (optional)

Yarn sewing needle

Large-eyed embroidery needle

SIZE

To fit a child 7–9 (10–12) years

(For more information on sizes, see page 112)

Actual measurements: approx. 7½in/19cm (8¼in/21cm) from toe to heel (unstretched)

GAUGE (TENSION)

20 sts and 26 rows to 4in (10cm) square over stockinette (stocking) stitch on US7 (4.5mm) needles

ABBREVIATIONS

See page 127

Main sock

(Make 2)

Using set of US7 (4.5mm) needles, cast on 40(44) sts in A.

Round 1: [K2, p2] to end, placing marker on 1st st of round.

Rep round 1, 14 times more.

Break A and join in B.

Knit 52(54) rounds.

HEEL

Cont in B, k10(11), turn.

Break B and join in A.

Next row: P20(22), turn.

Work rem of heel on 20(22) sts just worked, leaving rem 20(22) sts for instep on stitch holder or spare needle.

Next row: [Sl1 pwise WYB, k1] to end.

Next row: Sl1 pwise, p to end.

Rep last 2 rows 9(10) times more.

Next row: K12(13), ssk, k1, turn. *(19/21 sts)*

Next row: Sl1 pwise, p5, p2tog, p1, turn. *(18/20 sts)*

Next row: Sl1 pwise, k to 1 st before gap, ssk, k1, turn. *(17/19 sts)*

Next row: Sl1 pwise, p to 1 st before gap, p2tog, p1, turn. *(16/18 sts)*

Rep last 2 rows once more. *(14/16 sts)*

Next row: Sl1 pwise, k to st before gap, ssk, turn.

Next row: Sl1 pwise, p to last 2 sts, p2tog. *(12/14 sts)*

Break yarn.

HEEL GUSSET

On needle 1: Using B, k across all heel sts and pick up and knit 10(11) sts up side of heel flap.

On needle 2: K all 20(22) instep sts.

On needle 3: Pick up and knit 10(11) sts up side of heel flap and k6(7) of heel sts. *(52/58 sts)*

Put marker on next st to mark beg of round.

Next round: On needle 1, k to last 3 sts, k2tog, k1; on needle 2, k all sts; on needle 3, k1, ssk, k to end. *(50/56 sts)*

Next round: Knit.

Rep last 2 rounds 5(6) times more. *(40/44 sts)*

FOOT

Knit 18(20) rounds.

TOE

Round 1: On needle 1, k to last 3 sts, k2tog, k1; on needle 2, k1, ssk, k to last 3 sts, k2tog, k1; on needle 3, k1, ssk, k to end. *(36/40 sts)*
Round 2: Knit.
Rep rounds 1–2 once more. *(32/36 sts)*
Round 5: On needle 1, k to last 3 sts, k2tog, k1; on needle 2, k1, ssk, k to last 3 sts, k2tog, k1; on needle 3, k1, ssk, k to end. *(28/32 sts)*
Rep round 5, 5(6) times more. *(8 sts)*
Break yarn, thread through rem sts, and secure.

Ear

(Make 4)
Using standard US5 (3.75mm) needles, cast on 10 sts in C.
Knit 8 rows.
Row 9: Inc, k3, m1, k2, m1, k2, inc, k1. *(14 sts)*
Knit 9 rows.
Row 19: [K2tog] to end. *(7 sts)*
Break yarn, thread through rem sts, and secure.

Topknot

(Make 2)
Using standard US5 (3.75mm) needles, cast on 8 sts in C.
Row 1: [Inc] 8 times. *(16 sts)*
Knit 7 rows.
Row 9: [K2tog] to end. *(8 sts)*
Row 10: [K2tog] to end. *(4 sts)*
Break yarn, thread through rem sts, and secure.

To make up

Fold the ear pieces in half lengthwise and join the side and top seams.
Fold the topknot pieces in half lengthwise and join the main seam, leaving the lower edge open. Stuff lightly.
Sew the ears and topknots in place using the photograph as a guide.
For the eyes, use D to work French knots (see page 124). Using the same yarn, work a coil of chain stitch (see page 124) for the nose.
Weave in all loose ends.

tiger socks

I fell in love with this golden orange yarn in an easy-care wool and acrylic mix and thought it would make a great pair of socks to pay homage to the world's largest species of cat. And did you know that no two tigers have the same pattern of stripes? Well, apart from these tiger socks, that is—though please feel free to make them a little different from each other if you prefer.

YARN AND MATERIALS
Lion Brand Wool-Ease (80% acrylic, 20% wool), 197yd (180m) per 3oz (85g) ball of worsted (Aran) yarn

    1(2) ball(s) in Gold 171 (A)

    1 ball in Black 153 (B)

Oddment of light worsted (DK) yarn in off-white (C)

NEEDLES AND EQUIPMENT
Set of 4 US7 (4.5mm) double-pointed knitting needles

Pair of US7 (4.5mm) knitting needles

Stitch holder (optional)

Yarn sewing needle

Large-eyed embroidery needle

SIZE
To fit a child 7–9 (10–12) years

(For more information on sizes, see page 112)

Actual measurements: approx. 6¼in/16cm (7¼in/18.5cm) from toe to heel (unstretched)

GAUGE (TENSION)
18 sts and 24 rows to 4in (10cm) square over stockinette (stocking) stitch on US7 (4.5mm) needles

ABBREVIATIONS
See page 127

Main sock
(Make 2)
Using set of US7 (4.5mm) needles, cast on 36(40) sts in A.
Round 1: [K1, p1] to end, placing marker on 1st st of round.
Round 2: [P1, k1] to end.
Rep rounds 1–2 once more.
Knit 14(18) rounds.
Leave A and join in B.
Knit 2 rounds.
Break B and use A.
Knit 6 rounds.
Leave A and join in B.
Knit 2 rounds.

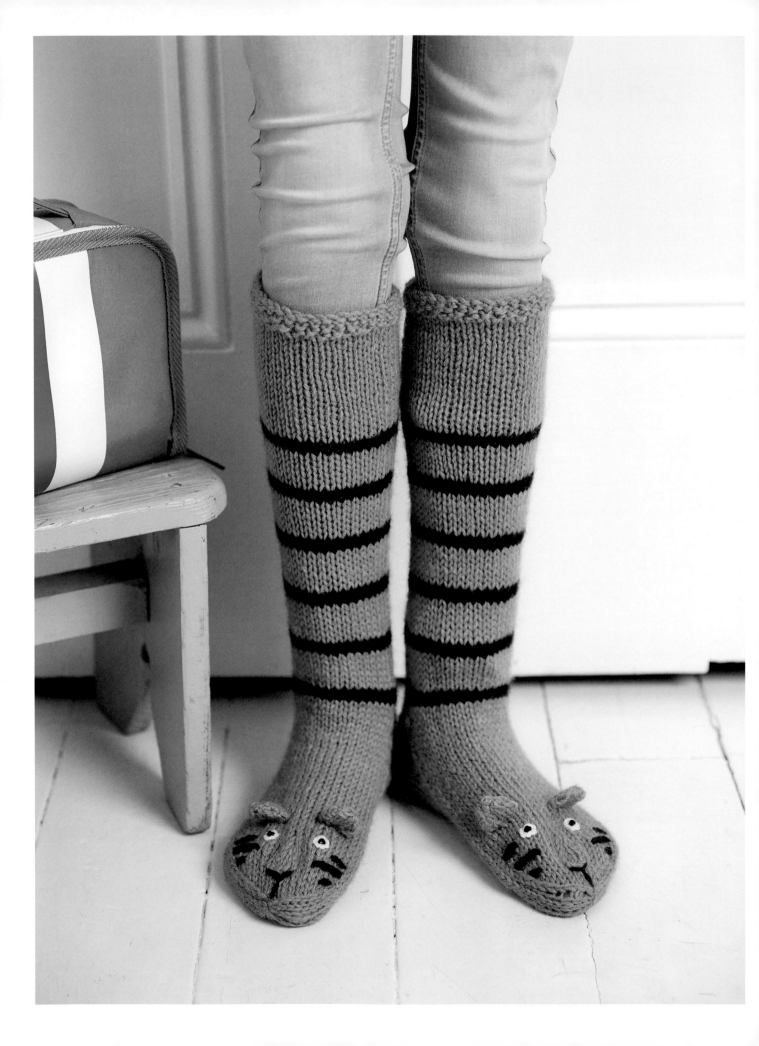

Break B.
Rep last 8 rounds 4 times more.
Work rem of sock in A.
Knit 3 rounds.

HEEL

Row 1: K9(10), turn.
Next row: P18(20), turn.
Work rem of heel on 18(20) sts just worked, leaving rem 18(20) sts for instep on stitch holder or spare needle.
Next row: [Sl1 pwise WYB, k1] to end.
Next row: Sl1 pwise, p to end.
Rep last 2 rows 8(9) times more.
Next row: K11(12), ssk, k1, turn.
Next row: Sl1 pwise, p5, p2tog, p1, turn.
Next row: Sl1 pwise, k to 1 st before gap, ssk, k1, turn.
Next row: Sl1 pwise, p to 1 st before gap, p2tog, p1, turn.
Rep last 2 rows once more. *(12/14 sts)*

Larger size only
Next row: Sl1 pwise, k to st before gap, ssk, turn.
Next row: Sl1 pwise, p to last 2 sts, p2tog. *(12 sts)*

HEEL GUSSET

On needle 1: K across all heel sts and pick up and knit 9(10) sts up side of heel flap.
On needle 2: K all 18(20) instep sts.
On needle 3: Pick up and knit 9(10) sts up side of heel flap and k6 of heel sts. *(48/52 sts)*
Put marker on next st to mark beg of round.
Next round: On needle 1, k to last 3 sts, k2tog, k1; on needle 2, k all sts; on needle 3, k1, ssk, k to end. *(46/50 sts)*
Next round: Knit.
Rep last 2 rounds 5 times more. *(36/40 sts)*

FOOT

Knit 12(16) rounds.

TOE

Round 1: On needle 1, k to last 3 sts, k2tog, k1; on needle 2, k1, ssk, k to last 3 sts, k2tog, k1; on needle 3, k1, ssk, k to end. *(32/36 sts)*
Round 2: Knit.
Rep rounds 1–2 once more. *(28/32 sts)*
Round 5: On needle 1, k to last 3 sts, k2tog, k1; on needle 2, k1, ssk, k to last 3 sts, k2tog, k1; on needle 3, k1, ssk, k to end. *(24/28 sts)*
Rep round 5, 4(5) times more. *(8 sts)*
Break yarn, thread through rem sts, and secure.

Ear

(Make 8)
Using standard US7 (4.5mm) needles, cast on 5 sts in A.
Work 3 rows in st st beg with a k row.
Row 4: P2tog, p1, p2tog tbl. *(3 sts)*
Row 5: K3tog. *(1 st)*
Fasten off.

To make up

Pair up ear pieces right sides together and oversew (see page 125) around curved edge, leaving the lower edges open for turning. Turn and close lower edges. Sew the ears in place using the photograph as a guide.
Using B, work French knots (see page 124) for the eyes.
Using C, work a circle of chain stitch (see page 124) around each eye.
Using B, work a Y-shape in straight stitch (see page 124) for the nostrils and cleft. Using A, work an elongated triangle shape in chain stitch for the nose.
Using B, work the facial stripes in chain stitch.
Weave in all loose ends.

marmalade cat hat

I love marmalade cats—also known as ginger cats—but I've only just discovered that their real name is "orange tabby." Whatever they're called, I think they're some of the loveliest felines around. But of course, you can knit this cat hat in any color you like, and the easy-care yarn I've chosen comes in a massive range of hues.

YARN AND MATERIALS
DMC Myboshi (70% acrylic, 30% wool), 60yd (55m) per 1¾oz (50g) ball of bulky (chunky) yarn

    1 ball in Neon Orange 181 (A)

    1 ball in Apricot 137 (B)

Oddment of light worsted (DK) yarn in mid-gray (C)

Oddment of light worsted (DK) yarn in white (D)

NEEDLES AND EQUIPMENT
Pair of US10 (6mm) knitting needles

2 x stitch markers or small safety pins

Yarn sewing needle

Large-eyed embroidery needle

SIZE
To fit a child 7–9 (10–12) years

(For more information on sizes, see page 112)

Actual measurements: approx. 18in/46cm (19¾in/50.5cm) circumference (unstretched)

GAUGE (TENSION)
13 sts and 18 rows to 4in (10cm) square over stockinette (stocking) stitch on US10 (6mm) needles

ABBREVIATIONS
See page 127

Main hat
(Make 1)

Cast on 60(66) sts in A, marking 22nd and 39th sts (24th and 43rd sts) with stitch markers or small safety pins.

Knit 4 rows.

Leave A at side and join in B.

Work 4 rows in st st beg with a k row.

Leave B at side and use A.

Work 2 rows in st st beg with a k row.

Rep last 6 rows, twice more.

Break A and work rem of hat in B.

Smaller size only

Next row: K4, [ssk, k8] 3 times, [k2tog, k8] twice, k2tog, k4. *(54 sts)*

Next and every WS row unless stated otherwise: Purl.

Larger size only

Work 2 rows in st st beg with a k row.

Next row: K4, [sl2, k1, p2sso, k8] 5 times, sl2, k1, p2sso, k4. *(54 sts)*

Next and every WS row unless stated otherwise: Purl.

Both sizes

Next RS row: K3, [sl2, k1, p2sso, k6] 5 times, sl2, k1, p2sso, k3. *(42 sts)*

Next RS row: K2, [sl2, k1, p2sso, k4] 5 times, sl2, k1, p2sso, k2. *(30 sts)*

Next RS row: K1, [sl2, k1, p2sso, k2] 5 times, sl2, k1, p2sso, k1. *(18 sts)*

Next row (WS): [P2tog] to end. *(9 sts)*

Break yarn leaving a long tail. Thread yarn tail through rem sts, pull up tightly, and secure.

Sew back seam of main hat using flat stitch (see page 126). With cast-on edge uppermost and RS facing, pick up and knit 22(24) sts from marked 22nd (24th) st to back seam, then pick up and knit another 22(24) sts from back seam to marked 39th (43rd) st. *(44/48 sts)*

Knit 5 rows.

Next row: K1, ssk, k to last 3 sts, k2tog, k1. *(42/46 sts)*

Next row: Knit.

Rep last 2 rows once more. *(40/44 sts)*

Bind (cast) off.

Ear

(Make 4)

Cast on 8 sts in B.

Work 4 rows in st st beg with a k row.

Row 5: K1, ssk, k2, k2tog, k1. *(6 sts)*

Row 6: Purl.

Row 7: K1, ssk, k2tog, k1. *(4 sts)*

Row 8: P2tog, p2tog tbl. *(2 sts)*

Row 9: Skpo. *(1 st)*

Fasten off.

To make up

Place two ear pieces together with right sides facing outward and seam along sides and lower edges. Stitch in place using the photograph as a guide.

Using C, work a small coil of chain stitch (see page 124) for eye centers and using D, work a circle of chain stitch around each eye center. Using C, work a coil of chain stitch for the nose and add curved lines in chain stitch for the mouth, using the photograph as a guide. Using a separated strand of C, work the whiskers in chain stitch. Weave in all loose ends.

whale hat

The blue whale is the largest creature on the planet and the largest animal to have ever existed, but here I've created a head-hugging miniature. For this project, you'll need to knit some small pieces for the fins, so it's not one for complete beginners. But if you've knitted a few hats already and feel ready to move on, then this project is a perfect challenge.

YARN AND MATERIALS
Katia Maxi Merino (55% wool, 45% acrylic), 137yd (125m) per 3½oz (100g) ball of bulky (chunky) yarn

    1 ball in 33 (A)

Oddment of light worsted (DK) yarn in black (B)

Oddment of light worsted (DK) yarn in white (C)

Small amount of polyester toy filling

NEEDLES AND EQUIPMENT
Pair of US9 (5.5mm) knitting needles

US G-6 (4mm) crochet hook or one of similar size

Yarn sewing needle

Large-eyed embroidery needle

SIZE
To fit a child 7–9 (10–12) years

(For more information on sizes, see page 112)

Actual measurements: approx. 18½in/47cm (20in/51cm) circumference (unstretched)

GAUGE (TENSION)
14 sts and 18 rows to 4in (10cm) square over stockinette (stocking) stitch on US9 (5.5mm) needles

ABBREVIATIONS
See page 127

Main hat
(Make 1)

Cast on 66(72) sts in A.

Row 1: [K1, p1] to end.

Row 2: [P1, k1] to end.

Rep rows 1–2 once more.

Work 22(24) rows in st st beg with a k row.

Larger size only

Next row: K5, [k2tog, k10] 5 times, k2tog, k5. *(66 sts)*

Next row: Purl.

Both sizes

Next row: K4, [sl2, k1, p2sso, k8] 5 times, sl2, k1, p2sso, k4. *(54 sts)*

Next and every WS row unless stated otherwise: Purl.

Next RS row: K3, [sl2, k1, p2sso, k6] 5 times, sl2, k1, p2sso, k3. *(42 sts)*

Next RS row: K2, [sl2, k1, p2sso, k4] 5 times, sl2, k1, p2sso, k2. *(30 sts)*
Next RS row: K1, [sl2, k1, p2sso, k2] 5 times, sl2, k1, p2sso, k1. *(18 sts)*
Next row (WS): [P2tog] to end. *(9 sts)*
Break yarn leaving a long tail. Thread yarn tail through rem sts, pull up tightly, and secure.

Fin A

(Make 2)
Cast on 9 sts in A.
Work 4 rows in st st beg with a k row.
Row 5: Ssk, k to last st, m1, k1.
Row 6: Purl.
Rep rows 5–6 once more.
Bind (cast) off.

Fin B

(Make 2)
Cast on 9 sts in A.
Work 4 rows in st st beg with a k row.
Row 5: K1, m1, k to last 2 sts, k2tog.
Row 6: Purl.
Rep rows 5–6 once more.
Bind (cast) off.

Tail

(Make 2)
Cast on 10 sts in A.
Work 4 rows in st st beg with a k row.
Row 5: K1, m1, k4, turn.
Work on 6 sts just worked, leaving rem sts on needle.
Work 3 rows in st st beg with a p row.
Next row: K1, m1, k to end. *(7 sts)*
Next and every WS row unless stated otherwise: Purl.
Next RS row: K1, m1, k to end. *(8 sts)*
Next RS row: K1, m1, k to end. *(9 sts)*
Next RS row: Ssk, k to last 2 sts, k2tog. *(7 sts)*
Next RS row: Ssk, k to last 2 sts, k2tog. *(5 sts)*
Next row: Bind (cast) off pwise.
Fasten off and rejoin yarn to rem 5 sts on RS of work.
Next row: K to last st, m1, k1. *(6 sts)*
Work 3 rows in st st beg with a p row.
Next RS row: K to last st, m1, k1. *(7 sts)*
Next and every WS row unless stated otherwise: Purl.
Next RS row: K to last st, m1, k1. *(8 sts)*
Next RS row: K to last st, m1, k1. *(9 sts)*
Next RS row: Ssk, k to last 2 sts, k2tog. *(7 sts)*
Next RS row: Ssk, k to last 2 sts, k2tog. *(5 sts)*
Next row: Bind (cast) off pwise.

Spout

Using the crochet hook and C, work eight 4-in (10-cm) crochet chains (see page 123).

To make up

Join back seam of hat using flat stitch (see page 126).
To make fin, seam one fin A piece to one fin B piece. Repeat to make the second fin. Stitch fins in place on side of hat.
To make tail, seam two tail pieces together, leaving cast-on edge open for stuffing. Stuff very lightly and stitch tail in place on back of hat, along upper and lower cast-on edges.
Using B, work a coil of chain stitch (see page 124) for the eye centers. Using a separated strand of A, work a circle of chain stitch around each eye center. Using B, work the mouth in chain stitch, using the photograph as a guide. For the blowhole, use A to work a small circle of chain stitch, approx. ⅜in (1cm) in diameter on the very top of the head. Weave in the yarn tails on one end of all the spout crochet chains. Sew the crochet chains in place using remaining yarn tails in the center of the blowhole. Sew the lower ½in (1.5cm) of the spouts together so it forms a semi-rigid stem.
Weave in all loose ends.

raccoon socks

These days, nimble-fingered raccoons feel as much at home in the city as the country. And they can eat pretty much anything, depending on what's around. I admit they can be a pesky nuisance if they shack up in your backyard , but I can't help thinking they're cool and rather smart. Just don't expect these raccoon socks to reform your fussy eater!

SKILL LEVEL

YARN AND MATERIALS
Sugar Bush Yarns Crisp (100% wool), 95yd (87m) per 1¾oz (50g) ball of light worsted (DK) yarn

    2 balls in Titanium 2018 (A)

    1 ball in Snowbird 2001 (B)

    1 ball in Lead 2019 (C)

Oddment of light worsted (DK) yarn in black (D)

4 x ⅜in (10mm) shiny black shank buttons

NEEDLES AND EQUIPMENT
Pair of US6 (4mm) knitting needles

Pair of US5 (3.75mm) knitting needles

Set of 4 US5 (3.75mm) double-pointed knitting needles

Stitch holder (optional)

Stitch marker

Yarn sewing needle

Large-eyed embroidery needle

Small nylon brush, such as a toothbrush (optional)

SIZE
To fit a child 7–9 (10–12) years

(For more information on sizes, see page 112)

Actual measurements: approx. 7in/18cm (8¼in/21cm) from toe to heel (unstretched)

GAUGE (TENSION)
22 sts and 28 rows to 4in (10cm) square over stockinette (stocking) stitch on US5 (3.75mm) needles

ABBREVIATIONS
See page 127

Main sock
(Make 2)

FRONT
(Make 1)
Using US6 (4mm) needles, cast on 22(24) sts in A.
Row 1: [K1, p1] to end.
Rep row 1, 3 times more.
Change to pair of US5 (3.75mm) needles.
Work next 14 rows from chart (overleaf).
Leave sts on one of the double-pointed needles.
Break yarns.

BACK
(Make 1)
Using US6 (4mm) needles, cast on 22(24) sts in A.
Row 1: [K1, p1] to end.
Rep row 1, 3 times more.
Change to pair of US5 (3.75mm) needles.
Work 14 rows in st st beg with a k row.
Break yarn.
Arrange front and back over 3 of the double-pointed needles, with the front on one needle and the back divided evenly between two needles and with right sides facing outward.
Join in A at mid-point of back of work and mark first st.
Knit 28(34) rounds.
Break yarn.

HEEL
Join in C.
Next row: K11(12), turn.
Next row: P22(24), turn.
Work rem of heel on 22(24) sts just worked, leaving rem 22(24) sts for instep on stitch holder or spare needle.
Next row: [Sl1 pwise WYB, k1] to end.
Next row: Sl1 pwise, p to end.
Rep last 2 rows 10(12) times more.
Next row: K13(14), ssk, k1, turn. *(21/23 sts)*
Next row: Sl1 pwise, p5, p2tog, p1, turn. *(20/22 sts)*

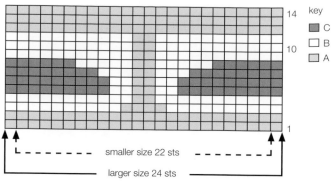

TOE

Round 1: On needle 1, k to last 3 sts, k2tog, k1; on needle 2, k1, ssk, k to last 3 sts, k2tog, k1; on needle 3, k1, ssk, k to end. *(40/44 sts)*

Round 2: Knit.

Rep rounds 1–2, 3 times more. *(28/32 sts)*

Round 9: On needle 1, k to last 3 sts, k2tog, k1; on needle 2, k1, ssk, k to last 3 sts, k2tog, k1; on needle 3, k1, ssk, k to end. *(24/28 sts)*

Rep round 9, 4(5) times more. *(8 sts)*

Break yarn, thread through rem sts, and secure.

Ear

(Make 4)

Using standard US5 (3.75mm) needles, cast on 6 sts in A.

Work 4 rows in st st beg with a k row.

Row 5: Ssk, k2, k2tog. *(4 sts)*

Row 6: P2tog, p2tog tbl. *(2 sts)*

Row 7: K2tog. *(1 st)*

Row 8: Inc pwise. *(2 sts)*

Row 9: [Inc] twice. *(4 sts)*

Row 10: [Inc pwise, p1] twice. *(6 sts)*

Work 3 rows in st st beg with a k row.

Bind (cast) off pwise.

To make up

Sew side seams at top of socks using flat stitch (see page 126).

Seam ear pieces together along sides and bottom.

Position ears on cast-on edge and stitch in place along front and back, using the photograph as a guide.

Sew buttons in place for eyes.

Using D, work a small coil of chain stitch (see page 124) for nose.

Weave in all loose ends.

Dampen ears and brush with small nylon brush to give a fluffy look.

Next row: Sl1 pwise, k to 1 st before gap, ssk, k1, turn. *(19/21 sts)*

Next row: Sl1 pwise, p to 1 st before gap, p2tog, p1, turn. *(18/20 sts)*

Rep last 2 rows twice more. *(14/16 sts)*

Larger size only

Next row: Sl1 pwise, k to last 2 sts, ssk, turn. *(15 sts)*

Next row: Sl1 pwise, p to last 2 sts, p2tog. *(14 sts)*

Both sizes

Break C and join in A.

HEEL GUSSET

On needle 1: K all heel sts and pick up and knit 11(12) sts up side of heel flap.

On needle 2: K all 22(24) instep sts.

On needle 3: Pick up and knit 11(12) sts up side of heel flap and k7 sts across heel. *(58/62 sts)*

Put marker on next st to mark beg of round.

Next round: On needle 1, k to last 3 sts, k2tog; on needle 2, k across all sts; on needle 3, k1, ssk, k to end. *(56/60 sts)*

Next round: Knit.

Rep last 2 rounds 6 times more. *(44/48 sts)*

FOOT

Knit 14(20) rounds.

Break A and join in C.

bat socks

Bats might not be the world's most noticeably cute creatures, but they are the world's only true flying mammal. I can't promise that these bat socks will help you make your way around in the dark, but the wool-rich, washable yarn in this lovely shade of charcoal will at least keep your feet looking good and feeling cozy.

YARN AND MATERIALS

Lion Brand Wool-Ease (80% acrylic, 20% wool), 197yd (180m) per 3oz (85g) ball of worsted (Aran) yarn

   1 ball in Oxford Grey 152 (A)

Oddment of light worsted (DK) yarn in black (B)

NEEDLES AND EQUIPMENT

Set of 4 US7 (4.5mm) double-pointed knitting needles

Pair of US7 (4.5mm) knitting needles

Stitch holder (optional)

Stitch marker

Yarn sewing needle

Large-eyed embroidery needle

SIZE

To fit a child 7–9 (10–12) years

(For more information on sizes, see page 112)

Actual measurements: approx. 7in/18cm (8¼in/21cm) from toe to heel (unstretched)

GAUGE (TENSION)

18 sts and 22 rows to 4in (10cm) square over stockinette (stocking) stitch on US7 (4.5mm) needles

ABBREVIATIONS

See page 127

Main sock

(Make 2)
Using set of US7 (4.5mm) needles, cast on 36(40) sts in A.
Round 1: [K2, p2] to end, placing marker on 1st st of round.
Rep round 1, 7(11) times more.
Knit 20 rounds.

HEEL
Row 1: K9(10), turn.
Next row: P18(20), turn.
Work rem of heel on 18(20) sts just worked, leaving rem 18(20) sts for instep on stitch holder or spare needle.
Next row: [Sl1 pwise WYB, k1] to end.
Next row: Sl1 pwise, p to end.
Rep last 2 rows 8(9) times more.
Next row: K11(12), ssk, k1, turn.

Next row: Sl1 pwise, p5, p2tog, p1, turn.
Next row: Sl1 pwise, k to 1 st before gap, ssk, k1, turn.
Next row: Sl1 pwise, p to 1 st before gap, p2tog, p1, turn.
Rep last 2 rows once more. *(12/14 sts)*

Larger size only

Next row: Sl1 pwise, k to st before gap, ssk, turn.
Next row: Sl1 pwise, p to last 2 sts, p2tog. *(12 sts)*

HEEL GUSSET

On needle 1: K across all heel sts and pick up and knit 9(10) sts up side of heel flap.
On needle 2: K all 18(20) instep sts.
On needle 3: Pick up and knit 9(10) sts up side of heel flap and k6 of heel sts. *(48/52 sts)*
Put marker on next st to mark beg of round.
Next round: On needle 1, k to last 3 sts, k2tog, k1; on needle 2, k all sts; on needle 3, k1, ssk, k to end. *(46/50 sts)*
Next round: Knit.
Rep last 2 rounds 5 times more. *(36/40 sts)*

FOOT

Knit 8(14) rounds.

TOE

Round 1: On needle 1, k to last 3 sts, k2tog, k1; on needle 2, k1, ssk, k to last 3 sts, k2tog, k1; on needle 3, k1, ssk, k to end. *(32/36 sts)*
Round 2: Knit.
Rep rounds 1–2 once more. *(28/32 sts)*
Round 5: On needle 1, k to last 3 sts, k2tog, k1; on needle 2, k1, ssk, k to last 3 sts, k2tog, k1; on needle 3, k1, ssk, k to end. *(24/28 sts)*
Rep round 5, 4(5) times more. *(8 sts)*
Break yarn, thread through rem sts, and secure.

Ear

(Make 4)
Using standard US7 (4.5mm) needles, cast on 5 sts in A.
Knit 3 rows.
Row 4: Ssk, k1, k2tog. *(3 sts)*
Row 5: Sl2, k1, p2sso. *(1 st)*
Fasten off.

Wings

(Make 4)
Using standard US7 (4.5mm) needles, cast on 33 sts in A.
Row 1: Purl.
Row 2: K4, [sl2, k1, p2sso, k8] twice, sl2, k1, p2sso, k4. *(27 sts)*
Row 3 and every WS row unless stated otherwise: Purl.
Row 4: K3, [sl2, k1, p2sso, k6] twice, sl2, k1, p2sso, k3. *(21 sts)*
Row 6: K2, [sl2, k1, p2sso, k4] twice, sl2, k1, p2sso, k2. *(15 sts)*
Row 8: K1, [sl2, k1, p2sso, k2] twice, sl2, k1, p2sso, k1. *(9 sts)*
Row 10: [Sl2, k1, p2sso] 3 times. *(3 sts)*
Row 11: P3tog. *(1 st)*
Fasten off.

To make up

Sew the ears in place using the photograph as a guide. Sew inner part of wing edge in place just behind the ears, using the photograph as a guide. Catch outer edge of wing in place on sides of socks.
Using B, work French knots (see page 124) for the eyes.
Weave in all loose ends.

cockatiel hat

I couldn't resist creating this hat, because of cockatiels' lovely soft colors. These birds originally come from Australia and, in the wild, you can see great flocks of them circling around looking for water. While it might be hard to knit a flock, I certainly think a pair could look pretty cute.

YARN AND MATERIALS

Cascade 128 Superwash (100% wool), 128yd (117m) per 3½oz (100g) ball of bulky (chunky) yarn

    1 ball in Lemon Drop 1984 (A)

Oddment of light worsted (DK) yarn in pale orange (B)

Oddment of light worsted (DK) yarn in black (C)

Oddment of light worsted (DK) yarn in mid-gray (D)

Very small amount of polyester toy filling

NEEDLES AND EQUIPMENT

Pair of US9 (5.5mm) knitting needles

Yarn sewing needle

Large-eyed embroidery needle

Small nylon brush, such as a toothbrush (optional)

SIZE

To fit a child 7–9 (10–12) years

(For more information on sizes, see page 112)

Actual measurements: approx. 17½in/44cm (18¾in/48cm) circumference (unstretched)

GAUGE (TENSION)

15 sts and 22 rows to 4in (10cm) square over stockinette (stocking) stitch on US9 (5.5mm) needles

ABBREVIATIONS

See page 127

Main hat

(Make 1)

Cast on 66(72) sts in A.

Row 1: [K1, p1] to end.

Rep row 1, 3 times more.

Work 22(24) rows in st st beg with a k row.

Larger size only

Next row: K5, [k2tog, k10] 5 times, k2tog, k5. *(66 sts)*

Next row: Purl.

Both sizes

Next row: K4, [sl2, k1, p2sso, k8] 5 times, sl2, k1, p2sso, k4. *(54 sts)*

Next and every WS row unless stated otherwise: Purl.

Next RS row: K3, [sl2, k1, p2sso, k6] 5 times, sl2, k1, p2sso, k3. *(42 sts)*

Next RS row: K2, [sl2, k1, p2sso, k4] 5 times, sl2, k1, p2sso, k2. *(30 sts)*

Next RS row: K1, [sl2, k1, p2sso, k2] 5 times, sl2, k1, p2sso, k1. *(18 sts)*

Next row (WS): [P2tog] to end. *(9 sts)*

Break yarn leaving a long tail. Thread yarn tail through rem sts, pull up tightly, and secure.

Crest

(Make 3)

Cast on 5 sts in A.

Row 1: K1, [yo, k2tog] twice.

Row 2: Purl.

Rep rows 1–2, 3 times more.

Row 9: Ssk, k1, k2tog. *(3 sts)*

Row 10: P3tog. *(1 st)*

Fasten off.

Beak

(Make 1)

Cast on 6 sts in D, using yarn double.

Work 4 rows in st st beg with a k row.

Row 5: K1, ssk, k2tog, k1. *(4 sts)*

Row 6: Purl.

Row 7: Ssk, k2tog. *(2 sts)*

Row 8: P2tog. *(1 st)*

Fasten off.

To make up

Join back seam of hat using flat stitch (see page 126). Fasten the three crest pieces in place along their cast-on edges at intervals of approx. ⅝in (1.5cm). The piece furthest from the front edge should be sewn at the very top of the hat.

Using B, work two large coils of chain stitch (see page 124) for the cheek patches, using the photograph as a position guide. Using C, work two small coils of chain stitch for the eyes. Sew beak in place using the photograph as a guide, stuffing very lightly as you go. Weave in all loose ends.

Using the small nylon brush, dampen then brush the crest lightly to give it a slightly fuzzy look.

CHAPTER 3

teens and grown-ups

sloth hat

It seems like everyone these days has fallen in love with sloths, those slow-moving creatures that hang upside down in the trees of Latin American rainforests. Perhaps it's their friendly nature, their cute faces, or just that they could teach us a thing or two about coping with 21st-century living. Whatever the reason, you can now join the sloth trend and knit your own cute hat. It's one of the easiest projects in the book, so there's really no excuse!

YARN AND MATERIALS

Katia Peru (40% wool, 40% acrylic, 20% alpaca), 115yd (106m) per 3½oz (100g) ball of bulky (chunky) yarn

  1 ball in 010 (A)
  1 ball in 007 (B)

Oddment of light worsted (DK) yarn in black (C)

NEEDLES AND EQUIPMENT

Pair of US9 (5.5mm) knitting needles

Pair of US8 (5mm) knitting needles

Yarn sewing needle

Large-eyed embroidery needle

4 x stitch markers or small safety pins

SIZE

To fit a small–medium (medium–large) teen to adult

(For more information on sizes, see page 112)

Actual measurements: approx. 17¾in/45cm (19in/48.5cm) circumference (unstretched)

GAUGE (TENSION)

16 sts and 19 rows to 4in (10cm) square over stockinette (stocking) stitch using US9 (5.5mm) needles

ABBREVIATIONS

See page 127

Main hat

(Make 1)

Using US9 (5.5mm) needles, cast on 72(78) sts in A. For smaller size only, mark the 9th, 24th, 49th, and 64th stitch with a stitch marker or small safety pin. For larger size only, mark the 11th, 26th, 53rd, and 68th.
Knit 4 rows.
Row 5: K30(33) in A, join in B and k12, k to end.
Row 6: P29(32) in A, p14 in B, p in A to end.
Row 7: K28(31) in A, k16 in B, k in A to end.
Row 8: P27(30) in A, p18 in B, p in A to end.
Row 9: K26(29) in A, k20 in B, k in A to end.
Row 10: P25(28) in A, p22 in B, p in A to end.
Row 11: K24(27) in A, k24 in B, k in A to end.
Work 7 rows in st st keeping to the patt set.
Row 19: K25(28) in A, k22 in B, k in A to end.
Row 20: P26(29) in A, p20 in B, p in A to end.
Row 21: K27(30) in A, k18 in B, k in A to end.
Row 22: P28(31) in A, p16 in B, p in A to end.
Break B and work rest of hat in A.

Smaller size only
Row 23: K5, [ssk, k10] 3 times, [k2tog, k10] twice, k2tog, k5. *(66 sts)*
Row 24: Purl.

Larger size only
Work 4 rows in st st beg with a k row.
Row 27: K5, [sl2, k1, p2sso, k10] 5 times, sl2, k1, p2sso, k5. *(66 sts)*
Row 28: Purl.

Both sizes
Next row: K4, [sl2, k1, p2sso, k8] 5 times, sl2, k1, p2sso, k4. *(54 sts)*
Next and every WS row unless stated otherwise: Purl.
Next RS row: K3, [sl2, k1, p2sso, k6] 5 times, sl2, k1, p2sso, k3. *(42 sts)*
Next RS row: K2, [sl2, k1, p2sso, k4] 5 times, sl2, k1, p2sso, k2. *(30 sts)*
Next RS row: K1, [sl2, k1, p2sso, k2] 5 times, sl2, k1, p2sso, k1. *(18 sts)*

Next row (WS): [P2tog] to end. *(9 sts)*
Break yarn leaving a long tail. Thread yarn tail through rem sts, pull up tightly, and secure.

Eye patches

(Make 2)
Using US8 (5mm) needles, cast on 5 sts in A.
Work 10 rows in st st beg with a k row.
Row 11: Ssk, k1, k2tog. *(3 sts)*
Row 12: P3tog. *(1 st)*
Fasten off.

Ear flaps

With RS facing and using US9 (5.5mm) needles and A, pick up and knit 16 sts between the first and second markers on the cast-on edge.
Knit 7 rows.

Row 8: Ssk, k to last 2 sts, k2tog. *(14 sts)*
Row 9: Knit.
Rep rows 8–9, 3 times more. *(8 sts)*
Row 16: Ssk, k4, k2tog. *(6 sts)*
Bind (cast) off.
Pick up and knit 16 sts between the third and fourth markers on the cast-on edge and work the second ear flap in the same way.

To make up

Oversew eye patches in place using the photograph as a guide.
Using C, work two small coils of chain stitch (see page 124) for the eyes and a bigger one for the nose. Using A, work the mouth in chain stitch.
Sew back seam using flat stitch (see page 126).
Weave in all loose ends.

llama socks

Who doesn't love a llama? They produce gorgeous yarn that's been made into textiles and clothes for hundreds of years. And with their brightly decorated halters and saddles, they carry heavy loads across the Andes mountains. I've knitted these socks in alpaca (which comes from the llama's smaller cousin) and added some bright pompoms as a nod to these fabulous creatures' South American heritage.

YARN AND MATERIALS

Berroco Folio DK (65% alpaca, 35% viscose), 218yd (200m) per 1¾oz (50g) ball of light worsted (DK) yarn

　　3 balls in Orr 4502 (A)

Oddment of light worsted (DK) yarn in black (B)

Oddments of light worsted (DK) yarn or yarn of similar weight for pompoms—you will need approx. ½yd (45cm) for each pompom, plus an extra few yards (meters) of the yarn used for the crochet tie

NEEDLES AND EQUIPMENT

Set of 4 US6 (4mm) double-pointed knitting needles

Set of 4 US5 (3.75mm) double-pointed knitting needles

Pair of US5 (3.75mm) knitting needles

USF-5 (3.75mm) crochet hook or one of similar size

Pompom maker to make 1¼in (3.5cm) pompoms, or four cardboard circles each measuring 1¼in (3.5cm) in diameter with a ½in (15mm) hole in the center

Stitch holder (optional)

Stitch marker

Yarn sewing needle

Large-eyed embroidery needle

SIZE

To fit a small (medium) teen to adult

(For more information on sizes, see page 112)

Actual measurements: approx. 8½in/22cm (9½in/24cm) from heel to toe (unstretched)

GAUGE (TENSION)

23 sts and 26 rows to 4in (10cm) square over stockinette (stocking) stitch on US5 (3.75mm needles) using yarn double

ABBREVIATIONS

See page 127

Main sock

(Make 2)

Using set of US6 (4mm) needles, cast on 44(48) sts in A, using yarn double.

Round 1: Knit
Round 2: Purl.
Round 3: Knit.
Round 4: Purl.
Knit 82(84) rounds.

HEEL

Next row: K11(12), turn.
Next row: P22(24), turn.
Work rem of heel on 22(24) sts just worked, leaving rem 22(24) sts for instep on stitch holder or spare needle.
Next row: [Sl1 pwise, k1] to end.
Next row: Sl1 pwise, p to end.
Rep last 2 rows 10(12) times more.
Next row: K13(14), ssk, k1, turn. *(21/23 sts)*
Next row: Sl1 pwise, p5, p2tog, p1, turn. *(20/22 sts)*
Next row: Sl1 pwise, k to 1 st before gap, ssk, k1, turn. *(19/21 sts)*
Next row: Sl1 pwise, p to 1 st before gap, p2tog, p1, turn. *(18/20 sts)*
Rep last 2 rows twice more. *(14/16 sts)*

Larger size only

Next row: Sl1 pwise, k to last 2 sts, ssk, turn. *(15 sts)*
Next row: Sl1 pwise, p to last 2 sts, p2tog. *(14 sts)*

Both sizes
HEEL GUSSET

On needle 1: K all heel sts and pick up and knit 11(12) sts up side of heel flap.
On needle 2: K all 22(24) instep sts.
On needle 3: Pick up and knit 11(12) sts up side of heel flap and k 7 sts across heel. *(58/62 sts)*
Put marker on next st to mark beg of round.
Next round: On needle 1, k to last 3 sts, k2tog; on needle 2, k across all sts; on needle 3, k1, ssk, k to end. *(56/60 sts)*

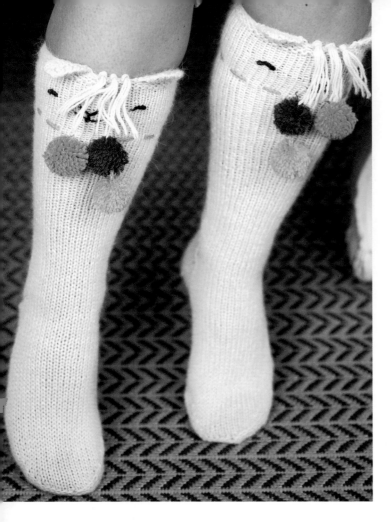

Next round: Knit.
Rep last 2 rounds 6 times more. *(44/48 sts)*

FOOT
Knit 22(28) rounds.

TOE
Round 1: On needle 1, k to last 3 sts, k2tog, k1; on needle 2, k1, ssk, k to last 3 sts, k2tog, k1; on needle 3, k1, ssk, k to end. *(40/44 sts)*
Round 2: Knit.
Rep rounds 1–2, 3 times more. *(28/32 sts)*
Round 9: On needle 1, k to last 3 sts, k2tog, k1; on needle 2, k1, ssk, k to last 3 sts, k2tog, k1; on needle 3, k1, ssk, k to end. *(24/28 sts)*
Rep round 9, 4(5) times more. *(8 sts)*
Break yarn, thread through rem sts, and secure.

Ear
(Make 4)
Using standard US5 (3.75mm) needles, cast on 8 sts in A.
Knit 6 rows.
Row 7: K1, ssk, k2, k2tog, k1. *(6 sts)*
Row 8: Knit.
Row 9: K1, ssk, k2tog, k1. *(4 sts)*
Row 10: Knit.
Row 11: Ssk, k2tog. *(2 sts)*
Row 12: K2tog. *(1 st)*
Fasten off.

Forelock
(Make 6 tassels)
Cut 4 x 5-in (13-cm) strands of A for each tassel.

Pompoms
Use the pompom maker or cardboard circles to make two pompoms in each of the three chosen colors.

Crochet tie
Using the crochet hook and chosen color, make two 13-in (33-cm) crochet chains (see page 123).

To make up
Stitch the ears in place.
Thread the crochet chain in and out of the sock from a point just to the left of the center front to a point just to the right of the center front. Thread the right-hand tie on one sock and the left-hand tie on the other through one pompom. Fasten the remaining pompoms to each end of the ties.
Using B, work two upside-down flattened U-shapes in chain stitch (see page 124). Again using B, work the nose and mouth in straight stitches (see page 124), using the photograph as a guide.
Use the crochet hook to create the forelock tassels, using the photograph as a guide.
Weave in all loose ends.

reindeer socks

Who wants boring store-bought socks for Christmas when you can create your own cozy reindeer versions? These socks are knitted in a bulky yarn so they don't take long to make. And, unlike most projects in the book, they're knitted flat on two needles. So if you're anxious about dipping your toe into the world of sock knitting, this pair is a great place to start.

YARN AND MATERIALS
Katia Peru (40% wool, 40% acrylic, 20% alpaca), 115yd (106m) per 3½oz (100g) ball of bulky (chunky) yarn

    1 ball in 010 (A)

    2 balls in 007 (B)

Oddment of bulky (chunky) or light worsted (DK) yarn in green (C)

Oddment of light worsted (DK) yarn in black (D)

Oddment of light worsted (DK) yarn in red (E)

NEEDLES AND EQUIPMENT
Pair of US10½ (6.5mm) knitting needles

Pair of US9 (5.5mm) knitting needles

US H-8 (5mm) crochet hook or one of similar size

Yarn sewing needle

Large-eyed embroidery needle

2 x stitch holders

SIZE
To fit a medium (large) teen or adult

(For more information on sizes, see page 112)

Actual measurements: approx. 9in/23cm (10in/25.5cm) from toe to heel (unstretched)

GAUGE (TENSION)
16 sts and 19 rows to 4in (10cm) square over stockinette (stocking) stitch using US9 (5.5mm) needles

ABBREVIATIONS
See page 127

Main sock

(Make 2)
Using US10½ (6.5mm) needles, cast on 34(38) sts in A.
Change to US9 (5.5mm) needles.
Knit 2 rows.
Break A and join in B.
Work 28(30) rows in st st beg with a p row.
Break yarn.

HEEL

With WS facing, put first 9(10) sts on first stitch holder and next 16(18) sts on second stitch holder for instep. *(9/10 sts on needle)*
With WS facing and US9 (5.5mm) needles, rejoin B to instep edge of 9(10) sts at end of row and purl to end, turn first stitch holder round and p9(10) sts. *(18/20 sts)*
Work on 18(20) sts just knitted, leaving instep sts on second stitch holder.

Work 14(16) rows in st st beg with a k row.
Next row: K10(11), ssk, k1, turn.
Next row: P4(3), p2tog, p1, turn.
Next row: K5(4), ssk, k1, turn.
Next row: P6(5), p2tog, p1, turn.
Next row: K7(6), ssk, k1, turn.
Next row: P8(7), p2tog, p1, turn.

Smaller size only

Next row: K to last 2 sts, ssk.
Next row: P to last 2 sts, p2tog. *(10 sts)*
Break yarn.

Larger size only

Next row: K8, ssk, k1, turn.
Next row: P9, p2tog, p1, turn.
Next row: Knit.
Next row: Purl. *(12 sts)*
Break yarn.

Both sizes
INSTEP

With RS facing and US9 (5.5mm) needles, rejoin B to right-hand side of heel flap and pick up and knit 10(11) sts up one side of heel, k across 10(12) sts of heel and pick up and knit 10(11) sts down other side of heel. *(30/34 sts)*
Next row: Purl.
Next row: K1, ssk, k to last 3 sts, k2tog, k1. *(28/32 sts)*
Work 3 rows in st st beg with a p row.
Rep last 4 rows, 5(6) times more. *(18/20 sts)*
Work 2 rows in st st beg with a k row.

TOE

*****Next row:** K1, ssk, k to last 3 sts, k2tog, k1. *(16/18 sts)*
Next row: Purl.
Next row: K1, ssk, k to last 3 sts, k2tog, k1. *(14/16 sts)*
Next row: P1, p2tog, p to last 3 sts, p2tog tbl, p1.
(12/14 sts)
Rep last 2 rows once more. *(8/10 sts)*
Leave sts on stitch holder or spare needle.*****
With WS facing and US9 (5.5mm) needles, rejoin B to 16(18) sts on stitch holder and p to end.
Next row: K1, m1, k to last st, m1, k1. *(18/20 sts)*
Work 25(29) rows in st st beg with a p row.
Rep from * to **.

Antler

(Make 4)
Using US9 (5.5mm) needles, cast on 9 sts in A.
Row 1: K4, [turn, k1] 5 times, turn, k3, [turn, k1] 5 times, turn, k to end.
Bind (cast) off.

Ear

(Make 4)
Using US9 (5.5mm) needles, cast on 4 sts in B.
Row 1: [Inc, k1] twice. *(6 sts)*
Row 2: K1, p to last st, k1.

Row 3: Knit.
Row 4: K1, p to last st, k1.
Rep rows 3–4 once more.
Row 7: Ssk, k2, k2tog. *(4 sts)*
Row 8: K1, p2, k1.
Row 9: Ssk, k2tog. *(2 sts)*
Row 10: K2tog. *(1 st)*
Fasten off.

Bow

(Make 2)
Using C (doubled if using light worsted/DK), crochet an 8½-in (22-cm) chain (see page 123).

To make up

Graft stitches using Kitchener stitch (see page 125) from both needles to join toe edge.
Join leg and foot seams of main socks.
Fold antlers lengthwise and slip stitch sides together.
Oversew antlers to top band of socks so that the "branches" point outward and the antlers are about 1¾in (4.5cm) apart.
Sew ears in place, using the photograph as a guide, with a distance of about 2½in (just over 6cm) between them.
For the eyes, use D to embroider a small coil in chain stitch (see page 124). For the nose, use E to embroider a slightly larger coil of chain stitch and add a vertical line in D, just beneath it.
Form the crochet chain into a bow and stitch in place, using the photograph as a guide.
Weave in all loose ends.

chameleon hat

With eyes that can swivel, never mind a body that can change color, chameleons have got to be one of the coolest creatures on the planet. And, with this hat, there's a good chance that you could look equally cool! Admittedly the hat won't actually change color, but the suggested yarn—a really comfortable wool-rich mix—comes in some fabulous shades.

YARN AND MATERIALS

Cascade Pacific Chunky (60% acrylic, 40% wool), 120yd (110m) per 3½oz (100g) ball of bulky (chunky) yarn

    1 ball in Spring Green 16 (A)

Rico Essentials Merino DK (100% wool), 131yd (120m) per 1¾oz (50g) ball of light worsted (DK) yarn

    1 ball in Green 42 (B)

Oddment of bulky (chunky) or light worsted (DK) yarn in white (C)

Oddment of bulky (chunky) or light worsted (DK) yarn in black (D)

Small handful of polyester toy filling

NEEDLES AND EQUIPMENT

Pair of US9 (5.5mm) knitting needles

Pair of US7 (4.5mm) knitting needles

Yarn sewing needle

Large-eyed embroidery needle

SIZE

To fit a small–medium (medium–large) teen to adult

(For more information on sizes, see page 112)

Actual measurements: approx. 17¾in/45cm (19in/48.5cm) circumference (unstretched)

GAUGE (TENSION)

16 sts and 18 rows to 4in (10cm) square over stockinette (stocking) stitch using US9 (5.5mm) needles

ABBREVIATIONS

See page 127

Main hat

(Make 1)

Using US9 (5.5mm) needles, cast on 70(78) sts in A.

Row 1: [K2, p2] to last 2 sts, k2.

Row 2: [P2, k2] to last 2 sts, p2.

Rep rows 1–2 once more, inc 2(0) sts evenly on last row. *(72/78 sts)*

Work 20(26) rows in st st beg with a k row.

Smaller size only

Row 25: K5, [ssk, k10] 3 times, [k2tog, k10] twice, k2tog, k5. *(66 sts)*

Row 26: Purl.

Larger size only

Row 31: K5, [sl2, k1, p2sso, k10] 5 times, sl2, k1, p2sso, k5. *(66 sts)*

Row 32: Purl.

Both sizes

Next row: K4, [sl2, k1, p2sso, k8] 5 times, sl2, k1, p2sso, k4. *(54 sts)*

Next and every WS row unless otherwise stated: Purl.

Next RS row: K3, [sl2, k1, p2sso, k6] 5 times, sl2, k1, p2sso, k3. *(42 sts)*

Next RS row: K2, [sl2, k1, p2sso, k4] 5 times, sl2, k1, p2sso, k2. *(30 sts)*

Next RS row: K1, [sl2, k1, p2sso, k2] 5 times, sl2, k1, p2sso, k1. *(18 sts)*

Next row (WS): [P2tog] to end. *(9 sts)*

Break yarn leaving a long tail. Thread yarn tail through rem sts, pull up tightly, and secure.

Ridge

(Make 2)

Using US9 (5.5mm) needles, cast on 3 sts in B, using yarn double.

[Bind/cast off 2 sts, slip rem st from RH to LH needle, cast on 2 sts] 23(29) times.

Bind/cast off.

Eye piece and eye

(Make 2)

Using US9 (5.5mm) needles, cast on 20 sts in A.

Work 4 rows in st st beg with a k row.

Break A.
Change to US7 (4.5mm) needles and join in C, using yarn double if using light worsted (DK).
Work 4 rows in st st beg with a k row.
Break C and join in D, using yarn double if using light worsted (DK).
Row 9: [K2tog] to end. *(10 sts)*
Row 10: [P2tog] to end. *(5 sts)*
Break yarn, thread yarn tail through rem sts, pull up tightly, and secure.

To make up

Sew back seam of main hat using flat stitch (see page 126).
Sew ridges in place beginning just above the ribbed edge on the front to the same point on the back and using the photograph as a guide.
Sew the back seams of the eye pieces and eyes using flat stitch.
Roll lower outside edge upward slightly and stuff remainder of eye part. Stitch in place.
Weave in all loose ends.

polar bear socks

The Arctic-dwelling polar bear is the biggest bear on the planet, and that's just one of the reasons I've created this pattern for those of us with medium-sized and larger feet. They're knitted in a gorgeous luxury yarn with a hint of mohair, so are guaranteed to keep your feet as warm as toast when it's icy outside.

YARN AND MATERIALS

Brown Sheep Lamb's Pride Bulky (85% wool, 15% mohair), 124yd (114m) per 4oz (113g) ball of bulky (chunky) yarn

> 2 balls in Crème M10 (A)

Oddment of light worsted (DK) yarn in dark gray (B)

NEEDLES AND EQUIPMENT

Pair of US11 (8mm) knitting needles

Pair of US10½ (6.5mm) knitting needles

Yarn sewing needle

Large-eyed embroidery needle

2 x stitch holders

SIZE

To fit a medium (large) teen or adult foot

(For more information on sizes, see page 112)

Actual measurements: approx. 10in/25cm (11½in/29cm) from toe to heel (unstretched)

GAUGE (TENSION)

12 sts and 16 rows to 4in (10cm) square over stockinette (stocking) stitch on US10½ (6.5mm) needles

ABBREVIATIONS

See page 127

Main sock

(Make 2)
Using US11 (8mm) needles, cast on 30(34) sts in A.
Change to US10½ (6.5mm) needles.
Row 1: Knit.
Work 24(28) rows in st st beg with a k row.
Break yarn.

HEEL

With WS facing, put first 8(9) sts on first stitch holder and next 14(16) sts on second stitch holder for instep.
(8/9 sts on needle)
With WS facing and US10½ (6.5mm) needles, rejoin yarn to instep edge of 8(9) sts at end of row and purl to end, turn first stitch holder around and p8(9) sts. *(16/18 sts)*
Work on 16(18) sts on needle only, leaving instep sts on second stitch holder.
Work 12(14) rows in st st beg with a k row.
Next row: K9(10), ssk, k1, turn.
Next row: P4, p2tog, p1, turn.
Next row: K5, ssk, k1, turn.
Next row: P6, p2tog, p1, turn. *(12/14 sts)*
Smaller size only
Next row: K7, ssk, k1.
Next row: P8, p2tog, p1. *(10 sts)*
Larger size only
Next row: K7, ssk, k1, turn.
Next row: P8, p2tog, p1, turn.
Next row: K9, ssk.
Next row: P9, p2tog. *(10 sts)*
Both sizes
Break yarn.

FOOT

With RS facing and US10½ (6.5mm) needles, rejoin yarn to right-hand side of heel flap and pick up and knit 9(10) sts up one side of heel, k across 10 sts of heel and pick up and knit 9(10) sts down other side of heel. *(28/30 sts)*
Next row: Purl.
Next row: K1, ssk, k to last 3 sts, k2tog, k1. *(26/28 sts)*
Work 3 rows in st st beg with a p row.
Rep last 4 rows, 5 times more. *(16/18 sts)*

Larger size only
Work 4 rows in st st beg with a k row.

TOE
*Next row: K1, ssk, k to last 3 sts, k2tog, k1. *(14/16 sts)*
Next row: Purl.
Next row: K1, ssk, k to last 3 sts, k2tog, k1. *(12/14 sts)*
Next row: P1, p2tog, p to last 3 sts, p2tog tbl, p1.
(10/12 sts)
Rep last 2 rows once more. *(6/8 sts)*
Leave sts on stitch holder or spare needle.**
With WS facing and US10½ (6.5mm) needles, rejoin A to
14(16) sts on stitch holder and p to end.
Next row: K1, m1, k to last st, m1, k1. *(16/18 sts)*
Work 23(27) rows in st st beg with a p row.
Rep from * to **.

Ear

(Make 2)
Using US10½ (6.5mm) needles, cast on 4 sts in A.
Work 2 rows in st st beg with a k row.
Row 3: Ssk, k2tog. *(2 sts)*
Row 4: P2tog. *(1 st)*
Row 5: Inc. *(2 sts)*
Row 6: [Inc pwise] twice. *(4 sts)*
Row 7: Knit.
Bind (cast) off kwise.

To make up

Graft stitches using Kitchener stitch (see page 125) from
both needles to join toe edge.
Join leg and foot seams of main socks.
Fold ears in half so that the right sides are facing outward
and sew around curved edges. Position ears on cast-on
edge and sew in place, using the photograph as a guide.
For the eyes, use B to embroider a small coil in chain stitch
(see page 124). For the nose, use B to embroider a larger
coil of chain stitch and add straight stitches (see page 124)
for the mouth beneath it, using the photograph as a guide.
Weave in all loose ends.

shark socks

Man-eating sharks aren't the cutest of creatures, but I thought man-eating socks would be cool—and I hope you agree. The socks are straightforward to knit, though you'll need to work a crochet edging and feel confident to make a knitted trim for the mouth and teeth. So while they're not a project for beginners, they'll be well within the reach of intermediate knitters, and well worth the effort.

YARN AND MATERIALS

Cascade 220 (100% wool), 218yd (200m) per 3½oz (100g) ball of worsted (Aran) yarn

   1(2) ball(s) in Grey 8509 (A)

Small amount of light worsted (DK) yarn in white (B)

4 x ⅜in (10mm) shiny black shank buttons

NEEDLES AND EQUIPMENT

Pair of US6 (4mm) knitting needles

Set of 4 US6 (4mm) double-pointed knitting needles

US G-6 (4mm) crochet hook or one of similar size

Stitch holder

Yarn sewing needle

Large-eyed embroidery needle

SIZE

To fit a small (medium) teen or adult

(For more information on sizes, see page 112)

Actual measurements: approx. 7¼in/18.5cm (8½in/22cm) from toe to heel (unstretched)

GAUGE (TENSION)

22 sts and 28 rows to 4in (10cm) square over stockinette (stocking) stitch on US6 (4mm) needles

ABBREVIATIONS

See page 127

Nose

(Make 4)

Using standard US6 (4mm) needles, cast on 2 sts in A.

Row 1: [Inc] twice. *(4 sts)*

Row 2: Purl.

Row 3: K1, m1, k to last st, m1, k1. *(6 sts)*

Row 4: Purl.

Rep rows 3–4, 9(10) times more. *(24/26 sts)*

Break yarn.

With RS of one nose piece facing, slip first 12(13) sts onto one of the dpns needles. With another of the needles and A, k next st and put marker on st to mark beginning of round then k rem 11(12) sts. With same needle and RS of second nose piece facing, k4(5) sts; with second needle, k16; with third needle k rem 4(5) sts from second nose piece and then k the slipped 12(13) sts. *(48/52 sts)*
Knit 30(34) rounds.

HEEL

Next row: K12(13), turn.
Next row: P24(26), turn.
Work rem of heel on 24(26) sts just worked, leaving rem 24(26) sts for instep on stitch holder or spare needle.
Next row: Sl1 pwise, k to end.
Next row: Sl1 pwise, p to end.
Rep last 2 rows 8 times more.
Next row: K14(15), ssk, k1, turn. *(23/25 sts)*
Next row: Sl1 pwise, p5, p2tog, p1, turn. *(22/24 sts)*
Next row: Sl1 pwise, k to 1 st before gap, ssk, k1, turn. *(21/23 sts)*
Next row: Sl1 pwise, p to 1 st before gap, p1, turn. *(20/22 sts)*

Rep last 2 rows 2(3) times more. *(16 sts)*
Next row: Sl1 pwise, k to last 2 sts, ssk, turn. *(15 sts)*
Next row: Sl1 pwise, p to last 2 sts, p2tog. *(14 sts)*

HEEL GUSSET

On needle 1: K all heel sts and pick up and knit 12 sts up side of heel flap.
On needle 2: K all 24(26) instep sts.
On needle 3: Pick up and knit 12 sts up side of heel flap and k7 sts across heel. *(62/64 sts)*
Put marker on next st to mark beg of round.
Next round: On needle 1, k to last 3 sts, k2tog, k1; on needle 2, k across all sts; on needle 3, k1, ssk, k to end. *(60/62 sts)*
Next round: Knit.
Rep last 2 rounds 6 times more. *(48/50 sts)*
Next round: On needle 1, k to last 3 sts, k2tog, k1; on needle 2, k2tog, k to last 2 sts, ssk; on needle 3, k1, ssk, k to end. *(44/46 sts)*

FOOT

Knit 16(22) rounds.

TOE

Round 1: On needle 1, k to last 3 sts, k2tog, k1; on needle 2, k1, ssk, k to last 3 sts, k2tog, k1; on needle 3, k1, ssk, k to end. *(40/42 sts)*
Round 2: Knit.
Rep rounds 1–2, once more. *(36/38 sts)*
Next round: On needle 1, k to last 3 sts, k2tog, k1; on needle 2, k1, ssk, k to last 3 sts, k2tog, k1; on needle 3, k1, ssk, k to end. *(32/34 sts)*
Rep last round, 6(7) times more. *(8/6 sts)*
Break yarn, thread through rem sts, and secure.

Fin

(Make 4)
Using standard US6 (4mm) needles, cast on 12 sts in A.
Row 1: Ssk, k to last 2 sts, k2tog. *(10 sts)*
Row 2: Purl.
Rep rows 1–2 twice more. *(6 sts)*
Row 7: Ssk, k2, k2tog. *(4 sts)*
Row 8: P2tog, p2tog tbl. *(2 sts)*
Row 9: K2tog. *(1 st)*
Fasten off.

Teeth

(Make 4)
Using standard US6 (4mm) needles, cast on 3 sts in B.
[Bind/cast off 2 sts, slip rem st from RH to LH needle, cast on 2 sts] 16 times.
Bind (cast) off.

To make up

Using crochet hook and A, work a crochet edging (see page 123) around mouth opening at top of sock. Sew teeth in place just inside mouth opening.
Using A, work 3 short curved rows of chain stitch for the gills (see page 124), using the photograph as a guide.
Sew black buttons for eyes in position.
Seam two fin pieces together along sides then stitch in place about halfway up sock, using the photograph as a guide.
Weave in all loose ends.

llama hat

If you fell in love with the llama socks on page 82, I think you'll love this llama hat, too. I've knitted it in an alpaca-rich yarn and, just like the socks, I've added a couple of bright pompoms for a bit of authenticity. Llamas actually come in a range of colors and although I've chosen off-white for this hat, it would also look great in camel or gray.

YARN AND MATERIALS

Berroco Ultra Alpaca Light (50% alpaca, 50% wool), 145yd (133m) per 1¾oz (50g) ball of light worsted (DK) yarn

    2 balls in Winter White 4201 (A)

Oddment of worsted (Aran) yarn in light blue (B)

Oddment of worsted (Aran) yarn in bright pink (C)

Oddment of light worsted (DK) yarn in dark gray (D)

Small amount of polyester toy filling

NEEDLES AND EQUIPMENT

Pair of US9 (5.5mm) knitting needles

Pair of US10½ (6.5mm) knitting needles

US K-10.5 (6.5mm) crochet hook or one of similar size

Yarn sewing needle

Large-eyed embroidery needle

4 x stitch markers or small safety pins

Pompom maker to make 1¾in (4.5cm) pompoms, or four cardboard circles each measuring 1¾in (4.5cm) in diameter with a ¾-in (18-mm) hole in the center

Small nylon brush, such as a toothbrush (optional)

SIZE

To fit a small–medium (medium–large) teen to adult

(For more information on sizes, see page 112)

Actual measurements: approx. 17¾in/45cm (19in/48.5cm) circumference (unstretched)

GAUGE (TENSION)

16 sts and 22 rows to 4in (10cm) square over stockinette (stocking) stitch on US9 (5.5mm) needles, using yarn double

ABBREVIATIONS

See page 127

Main hat

(Make 1)
Using US9 (5.5mm) needles, cast on 72(78) sts in A, using yarn double.
Mark the 8th, 23rd, 50th, and 65th sts (9th, 24th, 55th, and 70th sts) with stitch markers or small safety pins.
Knit 4 rows.
Work 22 rows in st st beg with a k row.

Smaller size only

Row 27: K5, [ssk, k10] 3 times, [k2tog, k10] twice, k2tog, k5. *(66 sts)*
Row 28: Purl.

Larger size only

Work 2 rows in st st beg with a k row.
Row 29: K5, [sl2, k1, p2sso, k10] 5 times, sl2, k1, p2sso, k5. *(66 sts)*
Row 30: Purl.

Both sizes

Next row: K4, [sl2, k1, p2sso, k8] 5 times, sl2, k1, p2sso, k4. *(54 sts)*
Next and every WS row unless stated otherwise: Purl.
Next RS row: K3, [sl2, k1, p2sso, k6] 5 times, sl2, k1, p2sso, k3. *(42 sts)*
Next RS row: K2, [sl2, k1, p2sso, k4] 5 times, sl2, k1, p2sso, k2. *(30 sts)*
Next RS row: K1, [sl2, k1, p2sso, k2] 5 times, sl2, k1, p2sso, k1. *(18 sts)*
Next row (WS): [P2tog] to end. *(9 sts)*
Break yarn leaving a long tail. Thread yarn tail through rem sts, pull up tightly, and secure.

Ear flaps

With RS facing and using US9 (5.5mm) needles and A double, pick up and knit 16 sts between the first and second markers on the cast-on edge.
Knit 5 rows.
Row 6: K1, ssk, k to last 3 sts, k2tog, k1. *(14 sts)*
Knit 3 rows.
Rep rows 6–9 (last 4 rows) twice more. *(10 sts)*

Row 18: K1, ssk, k to last 3 sts, k2tog, k1. *(8 sts)*
Row 19: Knit.
Rep rows 18–19 once more. *(6 sts)*
Row 22: K1, ssk, k2tog, k1. *(4 sts)*
Row 23: Ssk, k2tog. *(2 sts)*
Row 24: K2tog. *(1 st)*
Fasten off.
Pick up and knit 16 sts between the third and fourth markers on the cast-on edge and work the second ear flap in the same way.

Ear

(Make 4)
Using US9 (5.5mm) needles, cast on 8 sts in A, using yarn double.
Work 6 rows in st st beg with a k row.
Row 7: K1, ssk, k to last 3 sts, k2tog, k1. *(6 sts)*
Row 8: Purl.
Row 9: K1, ssk, k2tog, k1. *(4 sts)*
Row 10: Purl.
Row 11: Ssk, k2tog. *(2 sts)*
Row 12: P2tog. *(1 st)*
Fasten off.

Topknot

(Make 1)
Using US10½ (6.5mm) needles, cast on 5 sts in A, using yarn double.
Row 1: Inc, k to last 2 sts, inc, k1. *(7 sts)*
Row 2: Knit.
Rep rows 1–2 once more. *(9 sts)*
Knit 14 rows.
Bind (cast) off.

To make up

Sew back seam of the hat using flat stitch (see page 126). Place two ear pieces together with right sides facing outward and seam along sides and lower edges. Repeat to make second ear. Oversew (see page 125) the ears in position along the front and back of lower seam, using the photograph as a guide.
Using the photograph as a guide, sew topknot piece in position on top of head, so that cast-on edge lies between ears, stuffing very lightly as you go.
Using D, work two curved lines of chain stitch (see page 124) for eyes. Using the photograph as a guide, use D to work nose and mouth in chain stitch.
Using crochet hook and four strands of B, make two 3-in (8-cm) crochet chains (see page 123). Using pompom maker or cardboard circles and C, make two pompoms. Stitch one end of chain in place at the end of each ear flap and fasten a pompom to the other end.
Weave in all loose ends.
Using the small nylon brush, dampen then brush the topknot lightly to give it a slightly fuzzy look.

rabbit hat

If you want to rustle up a super-cute hat really quickly—or if you're a newbie knitter—this is definitely the project for you. It's knitted in a super bulky (super chunky) yarn, so won't take too long to create, and it's easy to put together. I loved this deep shade of lavender, but the yarn is also available in more neutral shades if you wanted your rabbit hat to be ever so slightly more subtle.

YARN AND MATERIALS
Plymouth Yarn Encore Mega (75% acrylic, 25% wool), 63yd (58m) per 3½oz (100g) ball of super bulky (super chunky) yarn

    2 balls in 1033 (A)

Oddment of light worsted (DK) yarn in black (B)

NEEDLES AND EQUIPMENT
Pair of US11 (8mm) knitting needles

Yarn sewing needle

Large-eyed embroidery needle

SIZE
One size fits most teens and adults

(For more information on sizes, see page 112)

Actual measurements: approx. 18¾in/48cm circumference (unstretched)

GAUGE (TENSION)
10 sts and 14 rows to 4in (10cm) square over stockinette (stocking) stitch on US11 (8mm) needles

ABBREVIATIONS
See page 127

Main hat
(Make 1)
Cast on 48 sts in A.
Work 18 rows in st st beg with a k row.
Row 19: [K6, k2tog] to end. *(42 sts)*
Next and every WS row until stated otherwise: Purl.
Next RS row: [K5, k2tog] to end. *(36 sts)*
Next RS row: [K4, k2tog] to end. *(30 sts)*
Next RS row: [K3, k2tog] to end. *(24 sts)*
Next RS row: [K2, k2tog] to end. *(18 sts)*
Next RS row: [K1, k2tog] to end. *(12 sts)*
Next row (WS): [P2tog] to end. *(6 sts)*
Break yarn leaving a long tail. Thread yarn tail through rem sts, pull up tightly, and secure.

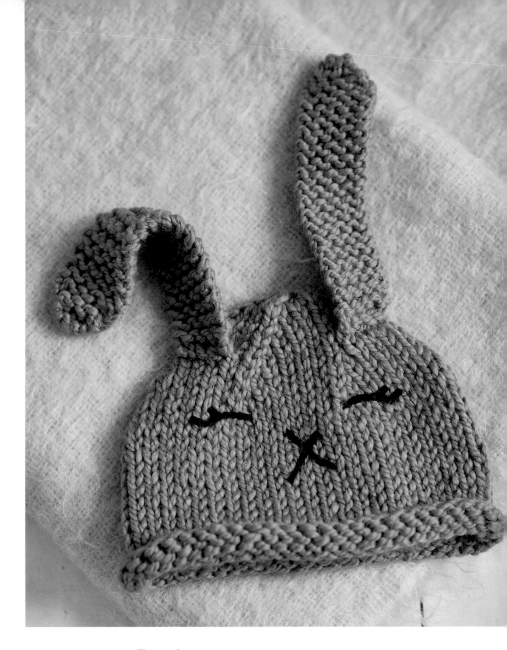

Ear

(Make 2)
Cast on 5 sts in A.
Knit 36 rows.
Row 37: Ssk, k3. *(4 sts)*
Row 38: Ssk, k2. *(3 sts)*
Row 39: Ssk, k1. *(2 sts)*
Row 40: K2tog. *(1 st)*
Fasten off.

To make up

Sew back seam of main hat using flat stitch (see page 126).
Stitch ears in place.
Using B, embroider eyes and nose in chain stitch (see page 124), using the photograph as a guide.
Weave in all loose ends.

bee hat

If you want to make a statement, bumblebee stripes are a great beginning and are sure to brighten a windy day. This hat is also one of the most straightforward projects in the book. I adore the soft wool-rich blend yarn, and while I also love the striking yellow-black combo, the yarn comes in a host of other equally dazzling shades. So take a peek and take your pick.

YARN AND MATERIALS

Cascade Pacific Chunky (60% acrylic, 40% wool), 120yd (110m) per 3½oz (100g) ball of bulky (chunky) yarn

   1 ball in Black 48 (A)

   1 ball in Gold 13 (B)

NEEDLES AND EQUIPMENT

Pair of US9 (5.5mm) knitting needles

Pompom maker to make 2½in (6.5cm) pompoms, or two cardboard circles each measuring 2½in (6.5cm) in diameter with a 1in (2.5cm) hole in the center

Yarn sewing needle

Large-eyed embroidery needle

SIZE

To fit a small–medium (medium–large) teen to adult

 (For more information on sizes, see page 112)

Actual measurements: approx. 17¾in/45cm (19in/48.5cm) circumference (unstretched)

GAUGE (TENSION)

16 sts and 20 rows to 4in (10cm) square over stockinette (stocking) stitch on US9 (5.5mm) needles

ABBREVIATIONS

See page 127

Main hat

(Make 1)

Cast on 72(78) sts in A.

Row 1: [K1, p1] to end.

Rep row 1, 17 times more.

Leave A at side and join in B.

Work 4 rows in st st beg with a k row.

Leave B at side and rejoin A.

Work 2 rows in st st beg with a k row.

Rep last 6 rows twice more.

Smaller size only

Leave A at side and rejoin B.

Row 37: K5, [ssk, k10] 3 times, [k2tog, k10] twice, k2tog, k5. *(66 sts)*

Row 38: Purl.

Next row: In B, k4, [sl2, k1, p2sso, k8] 5 times, sl2, k1, p2sso, k4. *(54 sts)*

Next and every WS row unless stated otherwise: Purl, keeping to color of previous row.

Next RS row: In A, k3, [sl2, k1, p2sso, k6] 5 times, sl2, k1, p2sso, k3. *(42 sts)*

Next RS row: In B, k2, [sl2, k1, p2sso, k4] 5 times, sl2, k1, p2sso, k2. *(30 sts)*

Next RS row: In B, k1, [sl2, k1, p2sso, k2] 5 times, sl2, k1, p2sso, k1. *(18 sts)*

Next row (WS): In B, [p2tog] to end. *(9 sts)*

Break yarn leaving a long tail. Thread yarn tail through rem sts, pull up tightly, and secure.

Larger size only

Leave A at side and rejoin B.

Work 4 rows in st st beg with a k row.

Row 41: In A, k5, [sl2, k1, p2sso, k10] 5 times, sl2, k1, p2sso, k5. *(66 sts)*

Row 42: Purl.

Row 43: In B, k4, [sl2, k1, p2sso, k8] 5 times, sl2, k1, p2sso, k4. *(54 sts)*

Next and every WS row unless stated otherwise: Purl, keeping to color of previous row.

Next RS row: In B, k3, [sl2, k1, p2sso, k6] 5 times, sl2, k1, p2sso, k3. *(42 sts)*

Next RS row: In A, k2, [sl2, k1, p2sso, k4] 5 times, sl2, k1, p2sso, k2. *(30 sts)*
Next RS row: In A, k1, [sl2, k1, p2sso, k2] 5 times, sl2, k1, p2sso, k1. *(18 sts)*
Next row (WS): In A, [p2tog] to end. *(9 sts)*
Break yarn leaving a long tail. Thread yarn tail through rem sts, pull up tightly, and secure.

To make up

Sew back seam of main hat using flat stitch (see page 126).
Using pompom maker or cardboard circles and A, make a pompom. Stitch pompom in place on top of hat.
Weave in all loose ends.

panda socks

Pandas normally live in the bamboo forests, high in the mountains of central China, but now you can create your very own pandas and have them living on your feet in your very own home. They're knitted in a 100 percent luxury wool yarn, which I thought would be perfect for these majestic creatures—and I think you'll love them!

YARN AND MATERIALS

Sublime Extra Fine Merino Worsted (100% wool), 109yd (100m) per 1¾oz (50g) ball of worsted (Aran) yarn

   2 balls in Alabaster 003 (A)

   2 balls in Jet Black 013 (B)

NEEDLES AND EQUIPMENT

Set of 4 US7 (4.5mm) double-pointed knitting needles

Pair of US7 (4.5mm) knitting needles

Stitch holder (optional)

Yarn sewing needle

Large-eyed embroidery needle

Small nylon brush, such as a toothbrush (optional)

SIZE

To fit a small (medium) teen to adult

(For more information on sizes, see page 112)

Actual measurements: approx. 8½in/22cm (9¾in/25cm) from heel to toe (unstretched)

GAUGE (TENSION)

20 sts and 26 rows to 4in (10cm) square over stockinette (stocking) stitch on US7 (4.5mm) needles

ABBREVIATIONS

See page 127

Main sock

(Make 2)

Using set of US7 (4.5mm) needles, cast on 48(52) sts in A.

Round 1: Knit
Round 2: Purl.
Round 3: Knit.
Round 4: Purl.
Knit 18 rounds.
Break A and join in B.
Knit 10 rounds.
Break B and join in A.
Knit 28 rounds.

HEEL

Next row: K12(13), turn.
Next row: P24(26), turn.
Work rem of heel on 24(26) sts just worked, leaving rem 24(26) sts for instep on stitch holder or spare needle.
Next row: [Sl1 pwise WYB, k1] to end.
Next row: Sl1 pwise, p to end.
Rep last 2 rows 10 times more.
Next row: K14(15), ssk, k1, turn. *(23/25 sts)*
Next row: Sl1 pwise, p5, p2tog, p1, turn. *(22/24 sts)*
Next row: Sl1 pwise, k to 1 st before gap, ssk, k1, turn. *(21/23 sts)*
Next row: Sl1 pwise, p to 1 st before gap, p1, turn. *(20/22 sts)*
Rep last 2 rows 2(3) times more. *(16 sts)*
Next row: Sl1 pwise, k to last 2 sts, ssk, turn. *(15 sts)*
Next row: Sl1 pwise, p to last 2 sts, p2tog. *(14 sts)*
Break A.

HEEL GUSSET

On needle 1: Using B, k all heel sts and pick up and knit 12 sts up side of heel flap.
On needle 2: K all 24(26) instep sts.
On needle 3: Pick up and knit 12 sts up side of heel flap and k7 sts across heel. *(62/64 sts)*
Put marker on next st to mark beg of round.

Next round: On needle 1, k to last 3 sts, k2tog, k1; on needle 2, k across all sts; on needle 3, k1, ssk, k to end. *(60/62 sts)*
Next round: Knit.
Rep last 2 rounds 6 times more. *(48/50 sts)*

FOOT
Knit 21(27) rounds.

TOE
Round 1: On needle 1, k to last 3 sts, k2tog, k1; on needle 2, k1, ssk, k to last 3 sts, k2tog, k1; on needle 3, k1, ssk, k to end. *(44/46 sts)*
Round 2: Knit.
Rep rounds 1–2, twice more. *(36/38 sts)*
Round 7: On needle 1, k to last 3 sts, k2tog, k1; on needle 2, k1, ssk, k to last 3 sts, k2tog, k1; on needle 3, k1, ssk, k to end. *(32/34 sts)*
Rep round 7, 6(7) times more. *(8/6 sts)*
Break yarn, thread through rem sts, and secure.

Ear

(Make 4)
Using standard US7 (4.5mm) needles, cast on 6 sts in B.
Work 3 rows in st st beg with a p row.
Row 4: Ssk, k2, k2tog. *(4 sts)*
Row 5: P2tog, p2tog tbl. *(2 sts)*
Row 6: [Inc] twice. *(4 sts)*
Row 7: [Inc pwise, p1] twice. *(6 sts)*
Work 3 rows in st st beg with a k row.
Bind (cast) off pwise.

To make up

Fold the ears so the right side is on the outside and stitch around the curved sides and lower edges. Position ears on cast-on edge and sew in place, using the photograph as a guide.
For the eye patches, use B to work a coil of chain stitch (see page 124) in a slanting oval shape, using the photograph as a guide. Using A, add a French knot (see page 124) for the eye itself. Using B, work a small coil of chain stitch
for the nose and add a straight stitch (see page 124) for the mouth.
Using the small nylon brush, dampen then brush the ears and eye patches lightly to give them a slightly fuzzy look. Weave in all loose ends.

dachshund socks

These little dogs were originally bred as hunting dogs in Germany, and they're now one of the most popular breeds in the world. I've knitted these doggy socks with a striped "coat" and they turned out to be one of my very favorite projects in the book. And remember that dachshunds come in lots of interesting color combinations—so raid your yarn stash and knit your own true originals.

YARN AND MATERIALS

Bergere de France Barisienne (100% acrylic), 153yd (140m) per 1¾oz (50g) ball of light worsted (DK) yarn

 2 balls in Brousaille 54704 (A)

 1 ball in Bouton d'or 54697 (B)

 1 ball in Papeete 24953 (C)

 1 ball in Nerine 22183 (D)

 1 ball in Marron 246481 (E)

Oddment of light worsted (DK) yarn in black (F)

Very small oddment of light worsted (DK) yarn in white (G) (for sock with open eyes only)

NEEDLES AND EQUIPMENT

Set of 4 US7 (4.5mm) double-pointed knitting needles

Set of 4 US5 (3.75mm) double-pointed knitting needles

Pair of US5 (3.75mm) knitting needles

Stitch holder (optional)

Stitch marker

Yarn sewing needle

Large-eyed embroidery needle

SIZE

To fit a small (medium) teen to adult

(For more information on sizes, see page 112)

Actual measurements: approx. 7½in/19cm (8½in/22cm) from heel to toe (unstretched)

GAUGE (TENSION)

20 sts and 28 rows to 4in (10cm) square over stockinette (stocking) stitch on US5 (3.75mm) needles

ABBREVIATIONS

See page 127

Main sock

(Make 2)

Using set of US7 (4.5mm) needles, cast on 48(52) sts in A.
Change to set of US5 (3.75mm) needles.
Round 1: [K1, p1] to end.
Rep round 1, 9 times more.
Knit 21(25) rounds.
Break A and join in B.
Knit 6 rounds.
Break B and join in C.
Knit 6 rounds.

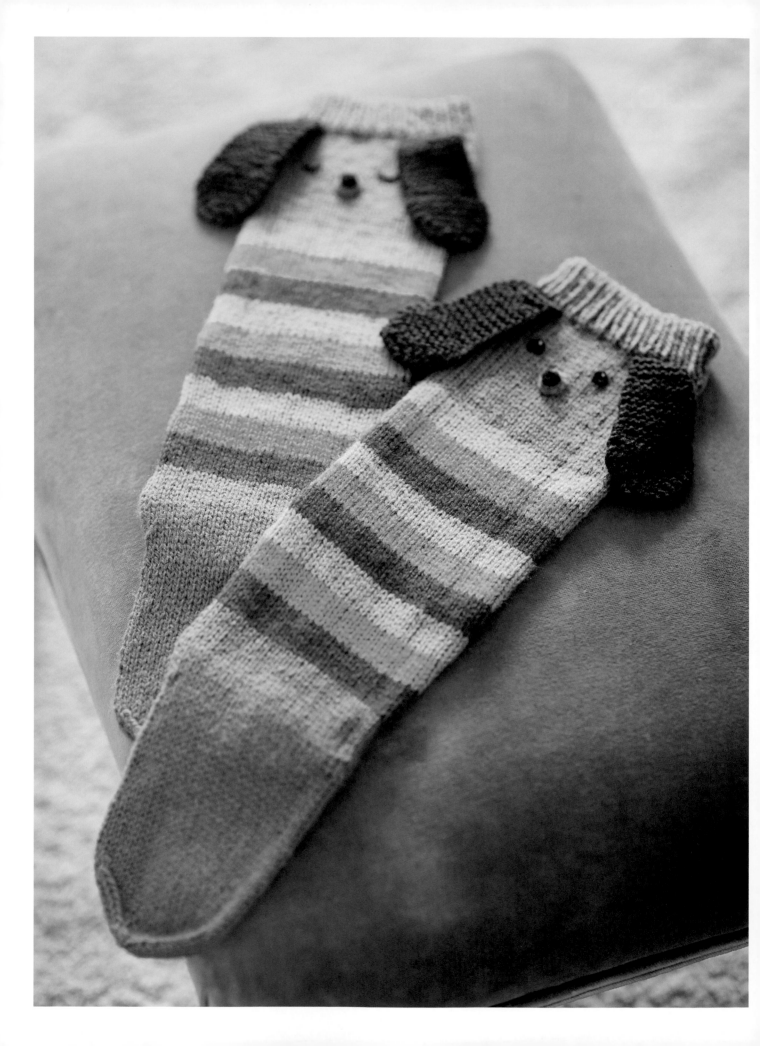

Break C and join in D.
Knit 6 rounds.
Rep this set of stripes (last 18 rounds) twice more.
Break D and join in A.

HEEL

Next row: K12(13), turn.
Next row: P24(26), turn.
Work rem of heel on 24(26) sts just worked, leaving rem 24(26) sts for instep on stitch holder or spare needle.
Next row: [Sl1 pwise WYB, k1] to end.
Next row: Sl1 pwise, p to end.
Rep last 2 rows 9(10) times more.
Next row: K14(15), ssk, k1, turn. *(23/25 sts)*
Next row: Sl1 pwise, p5, p2tog, p1, turn. *(22/24 sts)*
Next row: Sl1 pwise, k to 1 st before gap, ssk, k1, turn. *(21/23 sts)*
Next row: Sl1 pwise, p to 1 st before gap, p1, turn. *(20/22 sts)*
Rep last 2 rows 2(3) times more. *(16 sts)*
Next row: Sl1 pwise, k to last 2 sts, ssk, turn. *(15 sts)*
Next row: Sl1 pwise, p to last 2 sts, p2tog. *(14 sts)*

HEEL GUSSET

On needle 1: Using A, k all heel sts and pick up and knit 11(12) sts up side of heel flap.
On needle 2: K all 24(26) instep sts.
On needle 3: Pick up and knit 11(12) sts up side of heel flap and k7 sts across heel. *(60/64 sts)*
Put marker on next st to mark beg of round.
Next round: On needle 1, k to last 3 sts, k2tog, k1; on needle 2, k across all sts; on needle 3, k1, ssk, k to end. *(58/62 sts)*
Next round: Knit.
Rep last 2 rounds 5 times more. *(48/52 sts)*
Next round: On needle 1, k to last 3 sts, k2tog, k1; on needle 2, k2tog, k to last 2 sts, ssk; on needle 3, k1, ssk, k to end. *(44/48 sts)*

FOOT

Knit 20(26) rounds.

TOE

Round 1: On needle 1, k to last 3 sts, k2tog, k1; on needle 2, k1, ssk, k to last 3 sts, k2tog, k1; on needle 3, k1, ssk, k to end. *(40/44 sts)*
Round 2: Knit.
Round 3: On needle 1, k to last 3 sts, k2tog, k1; on needle 2, k1, ssk, k to last 3 sts, k2tog, k1; on needle 3, k1, ssk, k to end. *(36/40 sts)*
Rep round 3, 7(8) times more. *(8 sts)*
Break yarn, thread through rem sts, and secure.

Ear

(Make 4)
Using standard US5 (3.75mm) needles, cast on 7 sts in E.
Knit 6 rows.
Row 7: K2, m1, k3, m1, k2. *(9 sts)*
Knit 17 rows.
Row 25: K2, m1, k5, m1, k2. *(11 sts)*
Knit 7 rows.
Row 33: K1, ssk, k to last 3 sts, k2tog, k1. *(9 sts)*
Row 34: Knit.
Rep rows 33–34 once more. *(7 sts)*
Row 37: K1, ssk, k1, k2tog, k1. *(5 sts)*
Bind (cast) off.

To make up

For the open eyes, use F to work a small coil of chain stitch (see page 124) for each eye. Work a small straight stitch (see page 124) in G to add a highlight to the eye. For the closed eyes, use F to work a flattened U-shape in chain stitch. For the nose, work a slightly larger coil in chain stitch in F and work two circles of chain stitch around the nose in A.
Stitch the ears in place.
Weave in all loose ends.

zebra-striped socks

SKILL LEVEL

These zebra-striped socks are an ideal first sock project because they are knitted as straightforward tubes, with no heel shaping whatsoever. The tube design also means they'll fit a wide range of sizes. While I adore the black and white stripes, you could, of course, knit them in any color combination of your choice. So, if you've always been a bit reluctant about sock knitting, now you have no excuses.

YARN AND MATERIALS
Cascade 220 Superwash Merino (100% wool), 220yd (201m) per 3½oz (100g) ball of light worsted (DK) yarn

  1 ball in Black 28 (A)

  1 ball in White 25 (B)

NEEDLES AND EQUIPMENT
Set of 4 US7 (4.5mm) knitting needles

Set of 4 US6 (4mm) double-pointed knitting needles

Stitch marker

Yarn sewing needle

SIZE
To fit an average teen or adult

(For more information on sizes, see page 112)

Actual measurements: as these socks are tubes, there is no toe to heel measurement

GAUGE (TENSION)
22 sts and 26 rows to 4in (10cm) square over stockinette (stocking) stitch on US6 (4mm) needles

ABBREVIATIONS
See page 127

Main sock
(Make 2)
Using set of US7 (4.5mm) needles, cast on 48 sts in A. Switch to set of US6 (4mm) needles.
Round 1: [K2, p2] to end, placing marker on 1st st of round.
Rep round 1, 10 times more.
Leave A on inside of work. Join in B and k 6 rounds, twisting B and A before beginning each round so that A is held securely and is ready to work with when needed.
Leave B on inside of work. Using A, knit 6 rounds, twisting A and B before beginning each round so that B is held securely and is ready to work with when needed.
Rep last 12 rounds, 8 times more; or work to length required.
Work 6 rounds in B as before.
Break B and work remainder of sock in A.

TOE
Arrange work as follows: on needle 1, 12 sts; on needle 2, 24 sts; on needle 3, 12 sts.
Next round: On needle 1, k to last 3 sts, k2tog, k1; on needle 2, k1, ssk, k to last 3 sts, k2tog, k1; on needle 3, k1, ssk, k to end. *(44 sts)*
Next round: Knit.
Rep last 2 rounds 3 times more. *(32 sts)*
Next round: On needle 1, k to last 3 sts, k2tog, k1; on needle 2, k1, ssk, k to last 3 sts, k2tog, k1; on needle 3, k1, ssk, k to end. *(28 sts)*
Rep last round 5 times more. *(8 sts)*
Break yarn, thread through rem sts, and secure.

To make up
Weave in all loose ends.

techniques

On the following pages you'll find the basic knitting techniques that you will need for the patterns in this book.

sizes

Almost all the projects in this book can be knitted in two sizes. To help you choose which size to knit, here is a list of the measurements I've used to create the patterns. Remember that knitted items such as hats and socks are stretchy, so will fit a range of sizes. And for most of the socks in this book, you can easily make them longer or shorter in the foot or leg by knitting a few rows more or a few rows less.

HATS

Age group	Head circumference	
	in	cm
12–18 months	16	41
2–3 years	18	46
4–6 years	19	48
7–9 years	20	51
10–12 years	21	53
Small–medium teen/adult	22	56
Medium–large teen/adult	23	58

BOOTIES AND SOCKS

Age group	Shoe size		
	US	EU	UK
0–6 months	1–2	16–17	0–1
6–12 months	3	18	2
12–18 months	3½–5	19–20	2½–4
2–3 years	5½–9½	21–26	4½–8½
4–6 years	10–13	27–31	9–12
7–9 years	13½–3	32–34	12½–2
9–12 years	3½–4½	35–36	2½–3½
Small teen/adult	5–7	37–38	4–5½
Medium teen/adult	8–10½	39–41	6–8½
Large teen/adult	9½–11½	41–44	9–11

gauge (tension)

The gauge (tension) is the number of stitches and rows needed to produce a 4-in (10-cm) square of knitting.

Using the recommended yarn and needles, cast on 8 stitches more than the gauge (tension) instruction asks for. Work 8 rows (in pattern) more than needed. Bind (cast) off loosely. Lay the swatch flat without stretching it. Lay a ruler across the stitches with the 2in (5cm) mark centered on the knitting, then put a pin in the knitting at the 0 and at the 4in (10cm) marks. Count the stitches between the pins. Repeat this across the rows to count the number of rows to 4in (10cm).

If the number of stitches and rows counted is the same as the number asked for, you have the correct gauge (tension). If you do not have the same number then you will need to change your gauge (tension) by changing the size of your knitting needles. Use larger needles to get fewer stitches and smaller ones to get more stitches.

Do spend the time to achieve the gauge (tension) given with the pattern, or the sample you knit may turn out a different size to that expected.

You can substitute the yarn given in a pattern with the same weight of yarn in a different brand, but you will need to check the gauge (tension) to make sure the substitute yarn knits up to the same number of stitches per inch (centimeter). When calculating the quantity of substitute yarn you will need, it is the length of yarn in each ball that you need to check, rather than the weight of the ball; the length

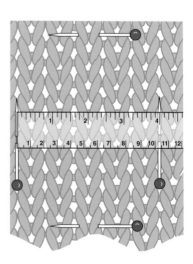

of yarn in each ball of the recommended project yarn is given in the materials list for that pattern.

holding needles

If you are a knitting novice, you will need to discover which is the most comfortable way for you to hold your needles.

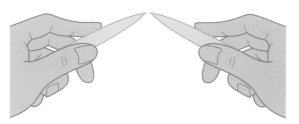

LIKE A KNIFE

Pick up the needles, one in each hand, as if you were holding a knife and fork—that is to say, with your hands lightly over the top of each needle. As you knit, you will tuck the blunt end of the right-hand needle under your arm, let go with your hand, and use your hand to manipulate the yarn, returning your hand to the needle to move the stitches along.

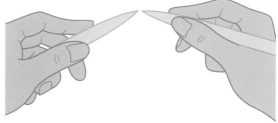

LIKE A PEN

Now try changing the right hand so you are holding the needle as you would hold a pen, with your thumb and forefinger lightly gripping the needle close to its pointed tip and the shaft resting in the crook of your thumb. As you knit, you will not need to let go of the needle but simply slide your right hand forward to manipulate the yarn.

holding yarn

As you knit, you work stitches off the left-hand needle onto the right-hand needle, and the yarn needs to be held and tensioned to produce even fabric. Use either your right or left hand, depending on the method you use to make stitches.

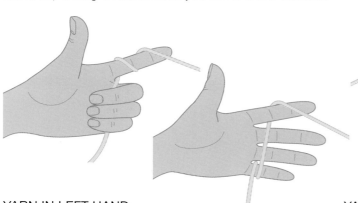

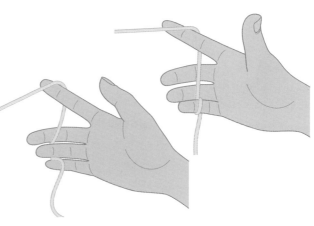

YARN IN LEFT HAND

To knit and purl in the Continental style (see pages 115 and 116), hold the yarn in your left hand. This method is sometimes easier for left-handed people to use, though many left-handers are quite comfortable knitting with the yarn in their right hand. Try the ways shown to find out which works best for you.

To hold the yarn tightly (above right), wind it right around your little finger, under your ring and middle fingers, then pass it over your index finger, which will manipulate the yarn.

For a looser hold (above left), fold your little, ring, and middle fingers over the yarn, and wind it twice around your index finger.

YARN IN RIGHT HAND

To knit and purl in the US/UK style (see pages 115 and 116), hold the yarn in your right hand. You can wind the yarn around your fingers in different ways, depending on how tightly you need to hold it to achieve an even gauge (tension). Try both ways shown to find out which works best for you.

To hold the yarn tightly (above right), wind it right around your little finger, under your ring and middle fingers, then pass it over your index finger, which will manipulate the yarn.

For a looser hold (above left), catch the yarn between your little and ring fingers, pass it under your middle finger, then over your index finger.

making a slip knot

You will need to make a slip knot to form your first cast-on stitch.

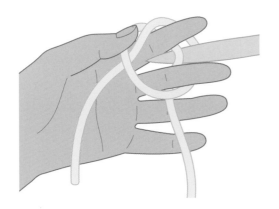

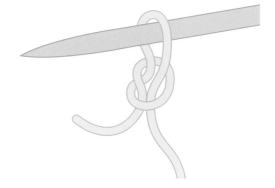

1 With the ball of yarn on your right, lay the end of the yarn on the palm of your left hand and hold it in place with your left thumb. With your right hand, take the yarn around your top two fingers to form a loop. Take the knitting needle through the back of the loop from right to left and use it to pick up the strand nearest to the yarn ball, as shown in the diagram. Pull the strand through to form a loop at the front.

2 Slip the yarn off your fingers, leaving the loop on the needle. Gently pull on both yarn ends to tighten the knot. Then pull on the yarn leading to the ball of yarn to tighten the knot on the needle.

casting on (cable method)

There are a few methods of casting on but the one used for the projects in this book is the cable method, which uses two needles.

1 Make a slip knot as shown above. Put the needle with the slip knot into your left hand. Insert the point of the other needle into the front of the slip knot and under the left-hand needle. Wind the yarn from the ball of yarn around the tip of the right-hand needle.

2 Using the tip of the needle, draw the yarn through the slip knot to form a loop. This loop is the new stitch. Slip the loop from the right-hand needle onto the left-hand needle.

3 To make the next stitch, insert the tip of the right-hand needle between the two stitches. Wind the yarn over the right-hand needle, from left to right, then draw the yarn through to form a loop. Transfer this loop to the left-hand needle. Repeat until you have cast on the right number of stitches for the project.

knit stitch

There are only two stitches to master in knitting; knit stitch and purl stitch. Most people in the English-speaking world knit using a method called English (or American) knitting. However, in parts of Europe, people prefer a method known as Continental knitting.

US/UK STYLE

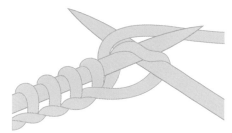 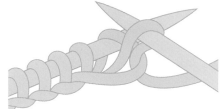 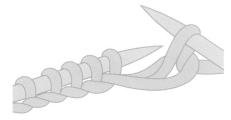

1 Hold the needle with the cast-on stitches in your left hand, and then insert the point of the right-hand needle into the front of the first stitch from left to right. Wind the yarn around the point of the right-hand needle, from left to right.

2 With the tip of the right-hand needle, pull the yarn through the stitch to form a loop. This loop is the new stitch.

3 Slip the original stitch off the left-hand needle by gently pulling the right-hand needle to the right. Repeat these steps till you have knitted all the stitches on the left-hand needle. To work the next row, transfer the needle with all the stitches into your left hand.

CONTINENTAL STYLE

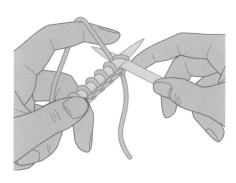 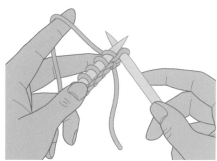 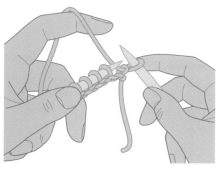

1 Hold the needle with the stitches to be knitted in your left hand, and then insert the tip of the right-hand needle into the front of the first stitch from left to right. Holding the yarn fairly taut with your left hand at the back of your work, use the tip of the right-hand needle to pick up a loop of yarn.

2 With the tip of the right-hand needle, bring the yarn through the original stitch to form a loop. This loop is the new stitch.

3 Slip the original stitch off the left-hand needle by gently pulling the right-hand needle to the right. Repeat these steps till you have knitted all the stitches on the left-hand needle. To work the next row, transfer the needle with all the stitches into your left hand.

purl stitch

As with knit stitch, purl stitch can be formed in two ways. If you are new to knitting, try both techniques to see which works better for you: left-handed people may find the Continental method easier to master.

US/UK STYLE

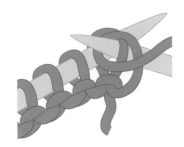  

1 Hold the needle with the stitches in your left hand, and then insert the point of the right-hand needle into the front of the first stitch from right to left. Wind the yarn around the point of the right-hand needle, from right to left.

2 With the tip of the right-hand needle, pull the yarn through the stitch to form a loop. This loop is the new stitch.

3 Slip the original stitch off the left-hand needle by gently pulling the right-hand needle to the right. Repeat these steps till you have purled all the stitches on the left-hand needle. To work the next row, transfer the needle with all the stitches into your left hand.

CONTINENTAL STYLE

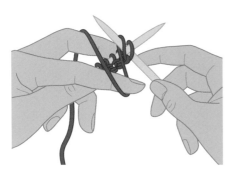  

1 Hold the needle with the stitches to be knitted in your left hand, and then insert the tip of the right-hand needle into the front of the first stitch from right to left. Holding the yarn fairly taut at the front of the work, move the tip of the right-hand needle under the working yarn, then push your left index finger downward, as shown, to hold the yarn around the needle.

2 With the tip of the right-hand needle, bring the yarn through the original stitch to form a loop.

3 Slip the original stitch off the left-hand needle by gently pulling the right-hand needle to the right. Repeat these steps till you have purled all the stitches on the left-hand needle. To work the next row, transfer the needle with all the stitches into your left hand.

binding (casting) off

You need to bind (cast) off the stitches to complete the projects and stop the knitting unraveling.

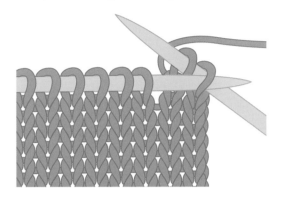

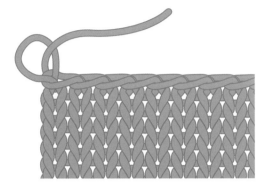

1 First knit two stitches in the normal way. With the point of the left-hand needle, pick up the first stitch you have just knitted and lift it over the second stitch. Knit another stitch so that there are two stitches on the right-hand needle again. Repeat the process of lifting the first stitch over the second stitch. Continue this process until there is just one stitch remaining on the right-hand needle.

2 Break the yarn, leaving a tail of yarn long enough to sew the work together (see page 125). Pull the tail all the way through the last stitch. Slip the stitch off the needle and pull it fairly tightly to make sure it is secure.

picking up stitches

For some projects, you will need to pick up stitches along either a horizontal edge (the cast-on or bound-/cast-off edge of your knitting), or a vertical edge (the edges of your rows of knitting).

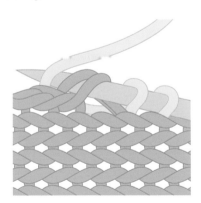

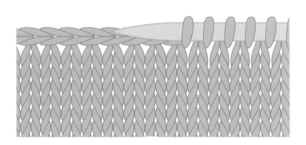

ALONG A ROW-END EDGE

With the right side of the knitting facing you, insert a knitting needle from the front to back between the first and second stitches of the first row. Wind the yarn around the needle and pull through a loop to form the new stitch. Normally you have more gaps between rows than stitches you need to pick up and knit. To make sure your picking up is even, you will have to miss a gap every few rows.

ALONG A CAST-ON OR BOUND- (CAST-) OFF EDGE

This is worked in the same way as picking up stitches along a vertical edge, except that you will work through the cast-on stitches rather than the gaps between rows. You will normally have the same number of stitches to pick up and knit as there are existing stitches.

slipping stitches

This means moving stitches from one needle to the other without knitting or purling them. They can be slipped knitwise or purlwise depending on the row you are working, or any specific pattern instructions.

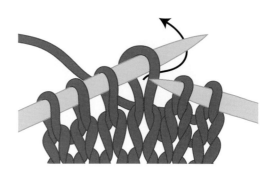

KNITWISE

From left to right, put the right-hand needle into the next stitch on the left-hand needle (as shown by the arrow) and slip it across onto the right-hand needle without working it.

PURLWISE

You can slip a stitch purlwise on a purl row or a knit row. From right to left, put the right-hand needle into the next stitch on the left-hand needle and slip it across onto the right-hand needle without working it.

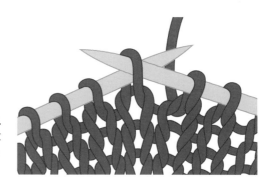

yarnover (yo)

To make a yarnover, wind the yarn around the right-hand needle to make an extra loop that is worked as a stitch on the next row.

Bring the yarn between the tips of the needles to the front. Take the yarn over the right-hand needle to the back and knit the next stitch on the left-hand needle (see page 115).

increasing

There are three methods of increasing used in projects in this book.

INCREASE ON A KNIT ROW (INC)

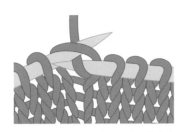

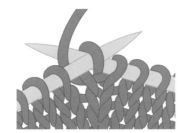

1 Knit the next stitch on the left-hand needle in the usual way (see page 115), but do not slip the "old" stitch off the left-hand needle.

2 Move the right-hand needle behind the left-hand needle and put it into the same stitch again, but through the back of the stitch this time. Knit the stitch again.

3 Now slip the "old" stitch off the left-hand needle in the usual way.

INCREASE ON A PURL ROW (INC PWISE)

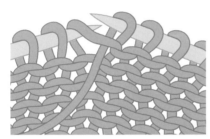

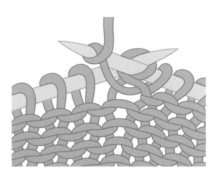

1 Purl the next stitch on the left-hand needle in the usual way (see page 116), but do not slip the "old" stitch off the left-hand needle.

2 Twist the right-hand needle backward to make it easier to put it into the same stitch again, but through the back of the stitch this time. Purl the stitch again, then slip the "old" stitch off the left-hand needle in the usual way.

MAKE ONE STITCH (M1)

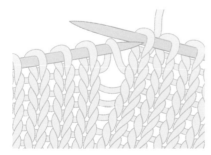

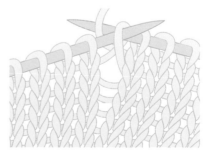

1 From the front, slip the tip of the left-hand needle under the horizontal strand of yarn running between the last stitch on the right-hand needle and the first stitch on the left-hand needle.

2 Put the right-hand needle knitwise into the back of the loop formed by the picked-up strand and knit into it in the normal way. (It is important to knit into the back of the loop so that it is twisted and a hole does not form in your work.)

decreasing

There are four different ways of decreasing used in this book, plus variations on some of the techniques.

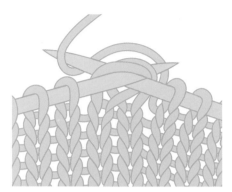

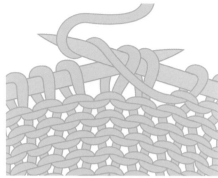

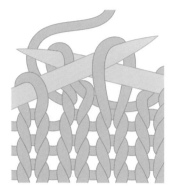

KNIT TWO TOGETHER (K2TOG)

This is the simplest way of decreasing. Simply insert the right-hand needle through two stitches instead of the normal one, and then knit them in the usual way (see page 115).

The same principle is used to knit three stitches together; just insert the right-hand needle through three stitches instead of through two.

PURL TWO TOGETHER (P2TOG)

To make a simple decrease on a purl row, insert the right-hand needle through two stitches instead of the normal one, and then purl them in the usual way (see page 116). To purl three stitches together, just insert the right-hand needle through three stitches instead of two.

This decrease can also be worked through the back of the stitch loops to make "p2tog tbl."

SLIP ONE, KNIT ONE, PASS THE SLIPPED STITCH OVER (SKPO)

Slip the first stitch knitwise from the left-hand to the right-hand needle without knitting it (see page 118). Knit the next stitch. Then lift the slipped stitch over the knitted stitch and drop it off the needle.

Another decrease that is worked in a similar way is sl2, k1, p2sso. Slip two stitches together, then knit one stitch, then one at a time, pass the slipped stitches over the knitted one.

SLIP, SLIP, KNIT (SSK)

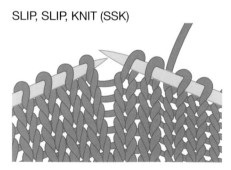

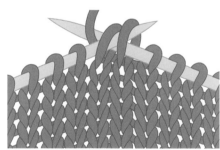

1 Slip one stitch knitwise, and then the next stitch knitwise onto the right-hand needle, without knitting them.

2 Insert the left-hand needle from left to right through the front loops of both the slipped stitches and knit them in the usual way.

knitting socks

There are many, many avid enthusiasts of sock knitting, who always have a sock on their needles and who try out every possible method of creating these favorite items. And there are beginner knitters for whom the very idea of knitting with more than two needles is horrifying—if this is you, then there are some pairs of socks in this book that are knitted on two needles so you can try those first. I've used a straightforward pattern for all the other socks in this book, and if you take your time and read the instructions carefully, you shouldn't have any problem creating your own knitted socks.

THE ANATOMY OF A SOCK

This diagram shows the various sections of the style of knitted sock used in this book, and how the sections relate to one another.

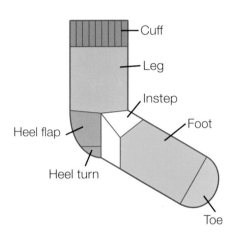

- Cuff
- Leg
- Instep
- Foot
- Heel flap
- Heel turn
- Toe

TURNING THE HEEL OF A SOCK

This is the part of a sock pattern that causes most concern among non-sock knitters. The patterns in this book use the traditional method of creating two separate elements: the heel flap and the actual turned heel. The heel flap is worked on only a section of the stitches; the others are held on needles not in use. After the heel flap is completed, a smaller heel is turned on the same stitches; the terminology refers to changing the direction of the knitting so that the foot lies at a 90° angle to the leg part. Turning the heel involves decreasing this group of stitches on either side so that a small central group of stitches is then joined to the held stitches, to continue as the instep and foot section.

KNITTING IN THE ROUND

You can knit seamless tubes by working round and round on double-pointed needles—usually called "dpns"—rather than back and forth on standard straight needles. This is one of those knitting techniques that looks terrifying, but isn't actually that hard to do; you just ignore all the needles other than the two you are working with. Practice the technique on scrap yarn if you haven't worked this way before.

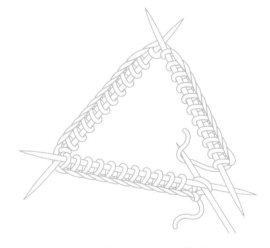

1 Divide evenly into three the number of stitches you need to cast on. Cast on (see page 114) to one needle one-third of the number of stitches needed, plus one extra stitch. Slip the extra stitch onto the second needle. Repeat the process, not forgetting to count the extra stitch, until the right number of stitches is cast on to each of the needles.

2 Arrange the needles in a triangle with the tips overlapping as shown here. Make sure that the cast-on edge is not twisted and place a round marker to keep track of the rounds. Pull the working tail of yarn across from the last stitch and using the free needle, knit the first stitch off the first needle (see page 115), knitting it firmly and pulling the yarn tight. Knit the rest of the stitches on the first needle, which then becomes the free one, ready to knit the stitches off the second needle. Knit the stitches off each needle in turn; when you get back to the marker, you have completed one round. Slip the marker onto the next needle and knit the next round.

knitting in different colors

It's important to change colors in the right way to keep the
knitted fabric flat and smooth and without any holes or gaps.

stranding

If you are knitting just a few stitches in a different color, you can simply leave the color you
are not using on the wrong side of the work and pick it up again when you need to.

CHANGING COLOR ON A KNIT ROW

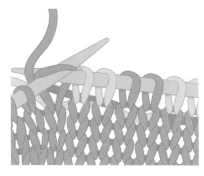 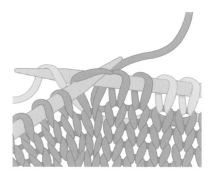

1 Knit the stitches (see page 115) in color A
(brown in this example), bringing the yarn
across over the strand of color B (lime in this
example) to wrap around the needle.

2 At the color change, drop color A and pick up color B, bringing it
across under the strand of color A to wrap around the needle. Be
careful not to pull it too tight. Knit the stitches in color B. When you
change back to color A, bring it across over the strand of color B.

CHANGING COLOR ON A PURL ROW

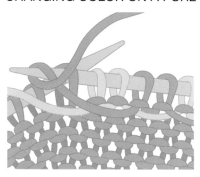 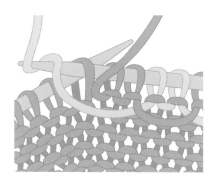

1 Purl the stitches (see page 116) in color A
(brown in this example), bringing it across over
the strand of color B (lime in this example) to
wrap around the needle.

2 At the color change, drop color A and pick up color B, bringing it
across under the strand of color A to wrap around the needle. Be
careful not to pull it too tight. Purl the stitches in color B. When you
change back to color A, bring it across over the strand of color B.

intarsia

If you are knitting blocks of different
colors within a project then you will
need to use a technique called
intarsia. This involves having separate
balls of yarn for each area and twisting
the yarns together where they join to
avoid creating a hole or gap.

ON THE RIGHT SIDE

When you want to change colors and
the color change is vertical or sloping
to the right, take the first color over
the second color. Then pick up the
second color, so the strands of yarn
cross each other.

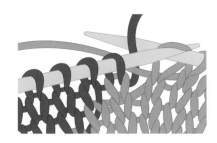

sewing seams

There are various sewing-up stitches, so do check pattern instructions for any specific advice.

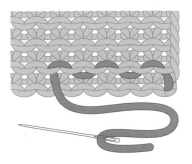

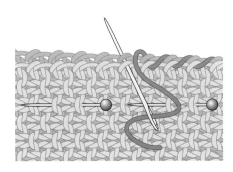

SEWING IN ENDS

The easiest way to finish yarn ends is to run a few small stitches forward then backward through your work, ideally in a seam. Use a pointed needle because working between the individual strands that make up the yarn can help the yarn tail stay put.

OVERSEWING

This stitch can be worked with the right or the wrong sides of the work together. Thread a yarn sewing needle with a tail left after binding (casting) off, or a long length of yarn. Bring the yarn from the back of the work, over the edge of the knitting, and out through to the back again a short distance further on.

KITCHENER STITCH

This is also called grafting, and is used in this book to sew up the toe of the socks knitted on two needles so that there isn't a lumpy seam. Arrange the two needles parallel with one another.

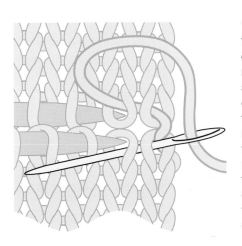

1 Measure out the working yarn to four times the width of the knitting, cut the yarn and thread a yarn sewing needle. From the back, bring the sewing needle through the first stitch of the lower piece and then, from the front, through the first stitch of the upper piece. Take the needle through the second stitch of the upper piece from the back, then from the front back through the first stitch of the lower piece. Bring it back to the front through the second stitch of the lower piece.

2 Continue in this pattern across the row, taking the sewing needle through a stitch from the front and then through the adjacent stitch on the same piece from the back. Take the needle across to the other piece of knitting and take it from the front through the stitch it last came out of, then through the back of the adjacent stitch on the same piece. Slide the knitting needles out of the knitted stitches as you join them.

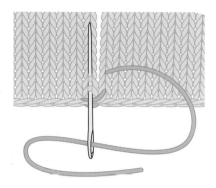

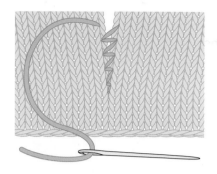

1 Right-sides up, lay the edges to be joined side by side. Thread a yarn sewing needle and from the back, bring it up between the first and second stitches of the left-hand piece, immediately above the cast-on edge. Take it across to the right-hand piece, and from the back bring it through between the first two stitches, immediately above the cast-on edge. Take it back to the left-hand piece and from the back, bring it through where it first came out. Pull the yarn through and this figure-eight will hold the cast-on edges level. Take the needle across to the right-hand piece and, from the front, take it under the bars of yarn between the first and second stitches on the next two rows up.

2 Take the needle across to the left-hand piece and, from the front, take it under the bars of yarn between the first and second stitches on the next two rows up. Continue in this way, taking the needle under two bars on one piece and then the other, to sew up the seam.

3 When you have sewn about 1in (2.5cm), gently and evenly pull the stitches tight to close the seam, and then continue to complete the sewing.

MATTRESS STITCH ON CAST-ON AND BOUND- (CAST-) OFF EDGES

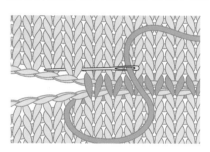

1 Right-sides up, lay the two edges to be joined side by side. Thread a yarn sewing needle with a tail left after binding (casting) off, or a long length of yarn. Secure the yarn on the back of the lower knitted piece, then bring the needle up through the middle of the first whole stitch in that piece. Take the needle under both "legs" of the first whole stitch on the upper piece, so that it comes to the front between the first and second stitches.

2 Go back into the lower piece and take the needle through to the back where it first came out, and then bring it back to the front in the middle of the next stitch along. Pull the yarn through. Take the needle under both "legs" of the next whole stitch on the upper piece. Repeat this step to sew the seam. Pull the stitches gently taut to close the seam as you work.

FLAT STITCH

Unlike mattress stitch, this stitch creates a join that is completely flat.
Lay the two edges to be joined side by side with the right side facing you. Using a yarn sewing needle, pick up the very outermost strand of knitting from one side and then the other, working your way along the seam and pulling the yarn up firmly every few stitches.

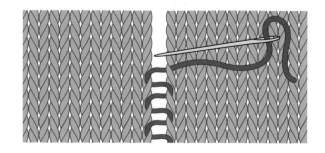

abbreviations

approx.	approximately
beg	begin(ning)
cm	centimeter(s)
cont	continue
g	gram(s)
in	inch(es)
inc	increase on a knit row, by working into front and back of next stitch: see page 119
inc pwise	increase on a purl row, by working into front and back of next stitch: see page 119
k	knit
k2tog	knit two stitches together: see page 120
k3tog	knit three stitches together: see page 120
kwise	knitwise
m1	make one stitch, by knitting into the strand between two stitches: see page 119
m	meter(s)
mm	millimeter
oz	ounces
p	purl
patt	pattern
p2tog	purl two stitches together: see page 120
psso	pass slipped stitch over: pass a slipped stitch over another stitch
p2sso	pass two slipped stitches over: pass two slipped stitches over another stitch
pwise	purlwise
rem	remain(ing)
rep	repeat
RS	right side
skpo	slip one stitch, knit one stitch, pass slipped stitch over knitted one, to decrease: see page 120
sl1(2)	slip one (two) stitch(es), from left- to right-hand needle without knitting it (them): see page 118.
ssk	slip one stitch, slip one stitch, knit slipped stitches together, to decrease: see page 120
st(s)	stitch(es)
st st	stockinette (stocking) stitch
tbl	through back loop: work through the back of the stitch
WS	wrong side
WYB	with yarn at back of work
yd	yard(s)
yo	yarnover: wrap yarn around needle between stitches, to increase and to make a hole: see page 118
[ ]	work instructions within square brackets as directed
*	work instructions after/between asterisk(s) as directed
( )	numbers within round brackets at the end of row instruction give the number of stitches there should be on the needle(s)

suppliers

For reasons of space we cannot cover all stockists, so please explore the local knitting shops and online stores in your own country.

USA

Knitting Fever Inc.
www.knittingfever.com

WEBS
www.yarn.com

Jo-Ann Fabric and Craft Stores
www.joann.com

UK

Love Knitting
www.loveknitting.com
Online sales

John Lewis
Retail stores and online
Tel: 03456 049049
www.johnlewis.com
Telephone numbers of stores on website

Laughing Hens
Online store only
Tel: +44 (0) 1829 740903
www.laughinghens.com

AUSTRALIA

Black Sheep Wool 'n' Wares
Retail store and online
Tel: +61 (0)2 6779 1196
www.blacksheepwool.com.au

Sun Spun
Retail store only (Canterbury, Victoria)
Tel: +61 (0)3 9830 1609

YARN COMPANIES

Cascade
www.cascadeyarns.com
Stockist locator on website

DMC
www.dmc.com
Stockist locator on website

Lion Brand
www.lionbrand.com

If you wish to substitute a different yarn for the one recommended in the pattern, try the **Yarnsub** website for suggestions:

www.yarnsub.com

index

author acknowledgments

My thanks to Cindy Richards, Penny Craig, Kerry Lewis, and the whole team at CICO Books for their good ideas and unstinting hard work. Thanks also to my editor Kate Haxell, my pattern checker Marilyn Wilson, photographer Terry Benson, and stylist Jess Contomichalos. I would also like to thank my sister Louise Turner for her help with the knitting and my husband Roger Dromard, who is beginning not to recognize me without knitting needles in my hands. Lastly, thanks to my mother Paddy Goble for supporting me when I did something different to what I'd planned.